Testosterone-Free Marketing™

The Yin and Yang of Marketing for Women

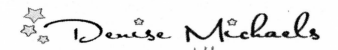

Denise Michaels

Testosterone-Free Marketing:
The Yin and Yang of Marketing for Women
by Denise Michaels

First printing: Spring 2005

ISBN: 1-891962-28-0

Published by:
Personal Transformation Press
8300 Rock Springs Road
Penryn, CA 95663
Phone: (916) 663-9178
Fax: (916) 663-0134

To order more copies of this book, please contact the publisher or the author at (702) 255-9119, or visit the author's website at www.marketingforher.com

Testosterone-Free Marketing™ is a Registered TradeMark of the author

Edited and designed by Tony Stubbs (www.tjpublish.com)

Printed in the United States of America

Table of Contents

Dedication iv
Acknowledgments v
Preface vi
1. From Pin Money to Economic Powerhouse 1
2. How an Unpaid Internship Led Me to Marketing Moolah 11
3. We Are Different –Thank Goodness for Small Miracles 21
4. Believe in Yourself and Your Vision 33
5. Courage, Like Love, Comes Straight from the Heart 47
6. Getting out of "Overwhelm" Forever 59
7. Thinking Bigger and Deserving Much More 71
8. Marketing Is Yang and Women Are Yin 83
9. Unleashing Your Feminine Force as a Marketer 97
10. Value Yourself and Your Business Highly 109
11. Zen Marketing and the Art of Detachment 121
12. Creating Balance and Support with Your Marketing Strategy ... 133
13. Marketing Strategies for Small Businesses 147
14. Your Power Pyramid for Success 161
15. About the Man in Your Life 175
16. Get in the Flow of Success 189

CDs and Tapes ....
About the Author ....

Dedication

To Ernie, the love of my life and the most supportive man in the world. Thank you, dear, from the bottom of my heart.

Acknowledgments

I want to acknowledge a few of the people who have been there for me on this road and provided their wisdom, support and love while writing this book. It's amazing how many people contribute to a journey of several years – each in their own unique way. Mostly the people who believed in me when I wasn't quite ready to believe in myself. Those are the people who awe and humble me at the same time. So, this list is in no particular order – as I think back to what a wonderful and challenging journey it has been.

To Robert Allen and Mark Victor Hansen, whose ebullient spirit, kindness, personal support and business brilliance has both dazzled and motivated me.

Great thanks for the support of Karen Nelson Bell, Duncan Guertin, Tom Painter, Trulene Hutchings, Bill Barnett, Robert Butwin, Jared Silver, Marlene Siersema, Sue Koch, Barbara Drazga, Elisabeth Baldazzi, Tamara Gilden, Steve Kiges, Maria Carter, John Childers, Janet Attwood, Chris Attwood, Teri Clark, Wade Thomas, Christina Daly, Gisela McKay, Bev Hanna, Althea Garner, Karl Helm, David Cooper, Laura Davis, John Eggen, Debbie Friedman, Bob Gatchel, David and Sonya Selley, Carl Turner and Scott LeTourneau.

Much gratitude to Art Martin, my publisher, at Personal Transformation Press and Tony Stubbs, my terrific editor. I'm thankful to Beth Sobiloff, web designer extraordinaire, Kaveri Sacheva Handa, my graphic designer, and Steven Boaze, Internet marketing genius and Christina Winsey-Rudd, the Ican Doctor.

And last but certainly not least, thanks to Donald and Joan Brozo, my parents. This book would never have taken place were it not for your contributions in my life.

Preface

It's crazy. Women are saying: "Enough! I'm mad as hell and I'm not gonna take it anymore." We're starting our own businesses at double the rate of men. More of us are becoming business owners than ever before. Unfortunately, many of you work hard but just don't make the money and create the cash you deserve.

If any of the following statements sound like you, then I wrote this book for you:

- You dreamed of a life of ease when you started your business, only to struggle financially.
- You want start your own business but are unsure how you'll ever get clients or customers.
- You would love to be a little more bold and confident, but without turning into the kind of shameless, brazen hussy who everyone hates.
- You have cut prices or given away products/services just "to be nice," but ended up hurting later.
- Your "better half" bugs you about when you're ever going to finally "get out there" with your business.
- You are enthusiastic and outgoing with people you know but a bit of a wimp when it comes to marketing or asking for the sale.
- You are convinced that your business deserves to succeed even though your results have been a little embarrassing.

I understand your frustration. Chances are you're good at what you do, but you never realized when you started your business what a big role marketing would play in keeping the money coming in. You thought if you were good or had a great product, business would flow in and everything would be fine. If it's not happening that way, you're like countless other women business owners.

For years, I wanted to get past the rough times and never struggle again. In the end, I did and today have a successful home-based business. Money flows in abundantly, and my savings grow every month. I do what I love every day. I live in a lovely home and travel in style. An assistant runs errands and helps me with other tasks, and a housekeeper keeps my home spotless and well organized two mornings a week. I never struggle. But there was a time when it wasn't so.

The truth is that the first time I ever marketed anything, I was nine years old. I was a Girl Scout and it was "cookie time." This was before grocery stores would let you set up a table outside. Or maybe my mom was too shy to do it with me. So I picked up her black vinyl phone book one evening after dinner and asked if I could call her friends to sell Girl Scout cookies. In two hours, I sold 36 boxes of cookies. I was thrilled but my mom was aghast. "You're being too direct. You're tooting your own horn too much. You can't just *call* people, exchange a little small talk and *ask* them if they would like to buy a box of cookies. That's way too forward. Way too bold. Go to your room."

Ashamed and embarrassed, I wondered what I had done that was so bad. My only "sin" was that I was a girl and in my mom's opinion, girls should never be so direct and just ask someone to buy something. My mom, who never sold anything in her life, thought I should "skirt around" and be indirect, and not just come out and *ask* for what I wanted. That was too straightforward and I was punished for not being a "nice girl."

I eventually finished school and worked in the corporate world for a few years … and hated it. I eventually started my own business but really struggled when it came to marketing. I hated getting the word out. Oh sure, I did it, but it was tough. I loved owning a business, but when I tried to make a sale or write an ad, it rarely turned out as I imagined but I couldn't figure out why. To make matters worse, I hated talking about myself or asking for the sale. I was discouraged and felt awful. The financial stress was a big factor, too. I wondered, why couldn't customers just come to me?

Then I discovered a secret … and another. As I worked with these discoveries, my life changed. The lights went on. Gradually more money came in. Over the years, I've been broke and I've been flush with money. Having money is better, believe me. And I developed a system so I could do it over and over. I fine-tuned it, tweaked it and tested it. In fact, I've coached over a thousand people, including 500 women like you to success.

Now, I'm so excited about this system I have to share it with you. I'm passionate about supporting women to go for their dreams and succeed. That's what this book is about. I want you to put more cash in your purse with less effort. After years of tweaking and testing, it's ready. I've cracked the code on why women experience challenges marketing their businesses that men don't, and what to do about it. No one else has this specialized information.

Face it: the guys are from Mars and we're from Venus. The "Testosterone Heavy" way doesn't work with our style, our personality or how we think and solve problems as a woman. We're different from men in some very fundamental ways.

You love your product or service. You don't mind talking about it in polite conversation. You want people to buy. But you wish someone else would get the word out for you. So you end up like millions of other women, slashing prices (and sometimes your self-esteem) to clients or customers. It's not what you had in mind when you started, is it?

When I talk about this book, people ask, "But, Denise, why just for women?" Here's the truth: We can actually market and sell better than men. We have more power than they do. We just have to learn the best ways to use it. With the techniques you learn about in this book, you can become a force of nature, have fun and turn your business into a cash machine.

Men approach marketing in ways that are fear-based and negative. They treat it as a "dog-eat-dog, all out war." In their version of marketing, for one man to succeed, another must fail. It's "warfare" this and "guerrilla" that. It's enough to make you want to go back to your office and work quietly while they get riled up and shoot to kill. One woman told me, "It's so macho that it makes my teeth ache."

We're different. We're women. We create the human race. We believe in win-win. We don't want to make all the money if someone else's children go hungry. And you know what? You can be successful, make lots of money *and* let others win. But you won't find the answers to doing that in testosterone-heavy marketing. They don't get it.

After a lot of missteps, I figured out the secrets to marketing success for women. I have a college degree in marketing and over a decade of successful experience helping entrepreneurs take their businesses from stagnant to sensational. I've helped people double their sales in two weeks. I've worked with business owners who have transformed their businesses from stressful, unprofitable and incompatible with their family life to businesses that give them more money and more time with family. You're in the right place.

I "get" marketing. From strategic planning and research to copywriting, the Internet, sales and public relations, I've done it all. For over four years, I've worked as a highly respected marketing trainer and coach with the most famous financial author in the USA. I'm the expert he hires to help his protégés succeed.

I've coached over 1,000 men and women, and discovered important secrets about the differences between the genders that will help you get the edge, market effectively and feel confident.

As a woman business owner, you'll break past your obstacles so you can claim and enjoy the success you deserve. As you read on, you'll be stunned when you discover how much usable, concrete, hands-on information you will get.

At one level, this book is a quick, easy read, so if it works for you, make a first pass through all the techniques to see where we're going, and then make a commitment to yourself to make a second pass, and do the exercises, make the lists, and put the techniques into practice. If you commit to as little as one chapter a week, at the end of four months, you will be a testosterone-free marketing expert.

So, on with the show …

Chapter One

From Pin Money to Economic Powerhouse

"It's the rooster that crows;

And the hen that delivers."

— Ann Richards, Former Governor of Texas

It's crazy.

Any woman who has run a household with children underfoot knows what it is to be married to a job, perhaps even more than a career-driven workaholic. Women are not new to work. I take offense with anyone who thinks a full-time homemaker has time to lie on the sofa, do her nails, and watch soap operas. Women have always worked.

Despite this, most of us are not generally known for our business prowess. As we entered the traditional workforce in the millions in the last few decades, we found that our skills as women, those greatly revered in the home, were not as appreciated in the rough and tumble world of male-dominated business.

Surprise! We Never Laid on the Sofa Eating Bonbons

The historic role of women has been overlooked and relegated to a short sentence here or there in the history books. Yet, from the beginning, women have worked to care for their children and husbands, and labor often to an early death to preserve them. Back in the days of the hunters and gatherers, women gathered and nurtured every day. They did not relax while the men hunted. They contributed fully and kept the family together.

Women spun wool and weaved cloth. We cooked, sewed and taught the children. Depending upon the culture, women sold pots, rugs and jewelry made in their own homes, or sold eggs from their own chickens. Women worked beside their husbands in the fields or the general store. Grandma and grandpa often lived under the same roof as Mom and Dad, watching the children and pitching in. People worked where they lived. Almost every family was a self-contained, home-based business. This was all before "the modern woman in the workforce" emerged.

The Industrial Revolution created enormous change in the Westernized world. As factories popped up, in Europe and North America, men were yanked out of the home. Since factory conditions were generally unsafe, they were considered an unfit environment for women. So, women still did what they had always done, plus they suddenly had to take on some of the "male" duties because the men were no longer around. We rose to the challenge as we always do.

In the 1930s, the United States was plunged into The Great Depression. Eventually our nation pulled out of its slump and companies prospered again. Men spent more time away from home. With social security and a pension, it was no longer necessary for the newly retired to move in with their grown children. Grandma and grandpa suddenly were moving to Florida and Sun City in droves.

During World War II, women poured into the factories and shipyards, making "Rosie the Riveter" a household name. Suddenly, a whole generation of us found that we could stand toe to toe with men and handle tough manufacturing jobs in what had been traditionally a man's world.

After the war, what about the mother with children? Her husband was away all day and her parents were off playing shuffleboard, available only for occasional babysitting. Once again, women's roles expanded. Never in history have women been afforded the opportunity to lie back and watch the world glide by. Not then, and definitely not now!

Check Your Soul at the Door

Is it any wonder women revolted in the sixties and seventies? Women were left with the jobs everyone else dumped. They watched our fathers dash away every day to their jobs. The world of careers and work must have looked mighty good to women back then.

We demanded and got increased rights and equal education. After generations of doing the work nobody else wanted, it was great to finally use our minds and start getting paid. We worked hard, hoping to get noticed and make progress up the corporate ladder. Sometimes it happened, but often it did not. Gradually, the edges of this liberated new world started crumbling.

For all our hard work and juggling, many of us checked our soul at the office door every morning. Even worse, it seemed as if we had to ignore our femininity and try to be like the guys to fit in. Pulling on a suit jacket with linebacker shoulder pads wasn't enough. After all, it was *their* world and *their* environment. The abyss grew between eons of social conditioning as women and who we were expected to be the minute we got to work and sat down at our desks.

To add insult to injury, we learned with sickening clarity about the glass ceiling as we watched men climb past us. Weren't we just doing what we were told? Why wasn't it working for us? There was something in this environment that men seemed comfortable with that made women feel incredibly uncomfortable. Like square pegs in round holes, many women felt completely out of their element.

Lorraine was a project manager in a large telecommunications company in San Diego, California. A mother of two junior high school age children, she worked hard to move up the ladder and still have a family life. When she walked in the door to her office every morning, she felt as if she always had to become someone she wasn't. The higher she moved up in the ranks, the more there was a "guy's locker room feel" her to work environment. The testosterone rose to the top. She worked hard to try to fit in and she was reasonably well liked. But at the end of the day, Lorraine always sighed with relief because she no longer had to be on guard and act like "one of the guys," playing a game that did not express her authentic self.

Millions of women have decided to chuck it all and go back home. Some women are going back to the traditional role of full-time wife and mother. Others are returning home to start our own businesses. With the ups and downs of our post-September 11 economy, many businesses are becoming less family-friendly to boot. We are finally deciding we have had enough of:

- **Inflexibility.** Whose idea was it to schedule a mandatory meeting at 4:30 pm when you have a nine-year-old to pick up from soccer practice at 5:15 pm?
- **The Glass Ceiling**. Gains have been made, but being overlooked and undervalued is still very real in the corporate arena for women.
- **The Daily Commute.** It can be enough to make you stressed-out the minute you walk in the door clutching your insulated coffee cup like a lifeline.
- **The Dress Code.** Sure it's fun to wear a suit sometimes, but who wouldn't mind ditching the daily pantyhose tussle for jeans and a cozy sweater.
- **Acting Like Someone You're Not**. 'Fess up. How many times have you had to feign interest in the Monday morning quarterback stories?
- **An Environment Designed for "Boys Playing Army."** Who came up with the title "Chief Operating Officer"? Should I salute?

According to a study by the Society of Human Resource Management of nearly 600 members, between 2001 and 2003, the percentage of employers offering paid family leave dropped from 27% to 23%. and job-sharing dropped from 26% to 22%. And from 2002 to 2003, employers offering flexible work hours fell from 64% to 55%.

Women start home-based businesses for many of the same reasons men do … well, except for that pantyhose thing. Both men and women start businesses because they want more time with their families. Both want the opportunity to determine their own destinies rather than sell their souls for the "Company Mission Statement."

Traditionally, the greatest spoils of the corporate world have gone to men. Naturally men have been slower to get off the fast track and start blazing new, entrepreneurial trails, but the last twenty years of corporate downsizing and other horrors have taught men it's no bed of roses for them either. Women also become business owners because we want to express who we are. Purpose suddenly matters more than ever, as we become more acutely aware of what is vital to us. Living a life congruent with who we are and how we think and feel is important. Women are strong, creative, intelligent, and resourceful—always have been and always will be. That's true whether we choose home in its traditional or non-traditional forms.

Years ago, women-run businesses were not looked upon as serious endeavors. Women and men trivialized them as for "pin money." Home and hearth was women's primary role. As women with impressive skills began businesses, some of those humble start-ups became viable enterprises contributing to our communities.

The groundswell of women business owners can be described as nothing short of phenomenal. Women lead the pack, starting home-based businesses at double the rate of men. Currently, women own 10.6 million businesses in America. Our businesses are an economic force to be reckoned with, as women currently control half of all US wealth and influence 80% of consumer spending decisions. Women-owned businesses now employ more people than the Fortune 500 worldwide. That's a lot of pins.

In 1977, Debbi Fields, a young California mother with no business experience, opened her first cookie store in Palo Alto. They told her she was crazy and that no business could survive just selling cookies. Today, she has 650 franchises in the U.S. and 65 in eleven nations worldwide.But it wasn't always easy. She went to 47 banks before one loaned her the money for her first cookie shop. She showed up at appointments with a tray of warm cookies. The bankers devoured the cookies … and then refused the loan.

It's a significant shift in the American workplace. We are saying, "I'm mad as hell and I'm not gonna take it anymore."

We also have earned rights that make our enterprises possible: our own money, checking accounts and credit. We buy homes, cars and build stock portfolios. We enter contracts and agreements unheard of one generation ago. I remember buying my first new car two months after graduating from college. It was 1980 and the dealer asked me to bring my father in to co-sign the loan. Dad suggested I ask them to approve the loan without it. I got my new car on my own. That was a big deal back then.

In our rush to freedom and business ownership, many women overlook the fact that marketing and sales are the most critical skills you will ever need to succeed. Doing the thing you excel at will buy you a job. A real business takes a balance of skills.

To get cash flow rolling in and create a business, you must find the best way to get the word out. Marketing will make your business blossom. Some skills required to get the word out might probably put you smack dab outside of your comfort zone right now. That's why you're reading this book. I felt the same way. Once you understand why women feel differently from men about marketing, you will discover ways to turn your former limitations around. You will learn to use your femininity to your advantage. And I will never ask you to attack and clobber the competition. There is much more about this in Chapter Eight. You can become an awesome marketer and build a wildly profitable business.

Choosing and Living the American Dream

The American Dream is still very much alive and well. All you have to do is take the time to learn how to get it. You don't have to give up your dream just because you, like millions of other women, do not enjoy getting out there and marketing. This book is about understanding yourself and taking positive steps forward, no matter what your past has been. Your failures can actually be the building blocks to your future success. You can have everything you imagined, whether it's money, freedom, the time to enjoy them with your family or even fame.

Testosterone-Free Marketing will help you become a more effective marketer and develop greater confidence. You will understand yourself and marketing on a different level than you knew existed. You will also learn that the way you were conditioned and raised as a girl was more disempowering than you ever realized. For all the changes that have taken place in the lives of women, little girls are still being raised and conditioned the same way. Once you get it, you will ask, "Gee, why did I make it so difficult on myself before?" (In addition to the enlightening, beneficial information in this book, you will find more resources available at www.MarketingForHer.com.)

The number of business tycoons who failed the first few times and then rose like the Phoenix from the ashes is awe-inspiring. If you have a business that's slumping along, take heart. If you are unsure if you should give it another go, fear not. Rags-to-riches stories have become part of the rich tapestry of Americana. Here are a couple of examples:

§ Mary Kay Ash didn't start her business until she was in her sixties and retired. Her retirement lasted less than a month, when she started Mary Kay Cosmetics.

§ J.K. Rowling was so poor that she worked on her book in a local coffee shop because she couldn't afford heat in her apartment. After the first Harry Potter book was published, she went on to become the wealthiest author of children's fiction in history.

In ***Testosterone-Free Marketing***, you will read stories of women who struggled and triumphed. Some had already owned businesses for fifteen years when we met. Others were just gathering information before taking the plunge. All were forthright enough to ask for help. I want to acknowledge you for purchasing this book. It says you are willing to do what it takes to go beyond what you know, and create a business that's fun and profitable, and fills your heart and your life.

Pull up a chair. It's time to talk about how ***Testosterone-Free Marketing*** will improve your life and your business. You will learn how to use your strengths as a woman to your advantage and create marketing that will put more money in your purse.

Summing It Up

§ Women are not new to work. We have always worked. We worked at home and in family businesses. We have stood with the people we love and often we have been on our own, bringing in the money and running our businesses.

§ Women now start home-based businesses for many of the same reasons men do. It's about financial freedom. We also start home-based businesses to spend more time with family and express ourselves creatively. You can have it all … but not when you sell your soul and your freedom to a company.

§ Women are starting home-based businesses at two to four times the rate of men. Currently, women own 10.6 million businesses in America.

§ Women control half of US wealth and influence 80 percent of consumer spending. Women-owned businesses employ more people than the Fortune 500 businesses.

Get Started Now

You stand at a crossroads: Do you want to continue your business as it has been, or are you looking to make marketing and attitude changes that will impact your business cash flow in a positive way? This book is about making positive changes. Make a commitment to your growth personally and professionally.

Write a Letter of Commitment to yourself. In this letter, state that you will finish reading this book by a specific date. Also state that you will complete the Action Steps at the end of each chapter. Finally, sign and date your letter. It is your commitment to yourself. Print it out and put it somewhere so you will see it every day until you have completed the ***Testosterone-Free Marketing*** program.

Last Word

The last three generations have seen amazing social changes, but we must avoid judging ourselves by men's "Testosterone-Heavy Scale." We are not better or worse, just *different.*

Chapter Two

How an Unpaid Internship Led Me to Marketing Moolah

There are three types of people in this world: those who make things happen, those who watch things happen and those who wonder what happened. We all have a choice. You can decide which type of person you want to be. I have always chosen to be in the first group.

— Mary Kay Ash

Despite my best efforts, I was not always successful at marketing. Through perseverance, tenacity and some great life lessons, I've learned valuable information that I want to share with everyone who chooses to read this book and take its lessons to heart.

When I was owned my first business, there were few women doing what I did. You are luckier; many, many women now own businesses. Yet, despite our growing numbers, many women still feel as uncomfortable about marketing themselves as I once did.

The Marble Desk Dream

I entered the world of marketing in my teens through an unpaid internship in Public Relations in high school. I didn't even know what "public relations" was back then, but it sounded sophisticated and glamorous. I learned fast. My second press release made the front page of the *Detroit Free Press*, one of the largest daily newspapers in America. I was thrilled and took a greater interest in advertising. I even started paying more attention to the ads on television than the programming.

My parents tried to discourage me. "How many want ads are there in the newspaper for jobs in advertising?" my mom asked. She was right; there weren't many listings. But back then the auto industry in Detroit was still a powerful economic force and the metropolitan area was tied with Chicago for third place in US advertising revenues.

In college, I read every issue of *Ad Week* in the library. I worked at the campus radio station, writing advertising copy and reading the news on the air. I dreamed of a corner office in a big advertising agency with an impressive marble desk. *Dynasty* was a popular TV show and someone on the show had a marble desk, I suppose.

I graduated with two majors: Business Marketing and Journalism/Advertising. I thought Business was the practical major and Journalism was the fun one. I've always been glad I have both.

Always Do What Excites You

When I graduated from college, I accepted a position as an advertising copywriter with one of the nation's largest retailers just a month before I got married. (That famous "Martha" still sells her sheets there.) I was 22. After coming home from a romantic honeymoon week, I settled into the start of my domestic life and my career.

The big corporate headquarters was a highly regimented place to work and I barely made over minimum wage. Everyone in the advertising copywriting department had a college degree, yet we still had to punch a time clock. I was bored, under-stimulated, and felt the world was passing me by. One day, I went in front of my boss and asked her about opportunities for advancement. She laughed hysterically. "Women don't advance in this company," she cackled. Obviously the company had a glass ceiling for women about the height of my coffee table. I started looking for ways to get out.

I bought a small business from my father-in-law and happily tendered my resignation. The repayment plan to my father-in-law appeared as if I would be paying him off forever. At least at age 24 it felt that way. However, that was not to be!

First Venture into Marketing My Own Business

The business was located in a cramped office in a sleepy town on the outskirts of Detroit—it was the local telephone answering service. The business stayed afloat because a cadre of doctors and other business people in the quaint burg insisted on getting their phone messages post haste, and answering machines had not caught on yet. Neither were voice mail, pagers, and cellular phones available. I had moved from an office in a huge, shiny complex to a dusty space with cheap paneling and dirty carpet, but at least I had more control over my destiny.

First, I looked for ways to cut expenses. I discovered the business was being over-charged by the phone company by one-third and the phone bill was the single largest monthly expense. The phone company overestimated the equipment we used for an entire year. They owed me a big fat credit plus lower phone bills from that point forward.

Next, I looked for ways to increase revenues. The monthly fee the business charged for the answering service had not been increased in five years. I increased the fee and assured every customer they would receive excellent service every time their line was answered. Not a single customer budged. With the money I made, I hired a part-time assistant.

Next, I went door-to-door to businesses in town with a flyer and sought out new clients. I had no idea what I was doing. I felt nervous, silly and odd walking into these little storefronts or offices and asking for the owner. Some wouldn't give me the time of day, and others were polite but the answer was "no." They weren't willing to use my business just because *I* thought it was a good idea. *They* had to believe it was a good idea, too. I had to figure out a way to make it seem in their best interests. I was both friendly and persistent.

Going door-to-door to these businesses never felt normal or comfortable. I always felt as if I was interrupting or imposing myself on people. The challenge was trying to find the right balance between being too aggressive and too subservient.

It never felt quite right, but slowly my efforts paid off. I would celebrate a new client with some small reward, but each time a new business opened or I met a business owner around town, it felt just as uncomfortable as day one. On the outside, it seemed as if my confidence was growing, but on the inside I was still as nervous as ever. This just didn't fit my picture of a glamorous, sophisticated entrepreneur. And I was no closer to getting a marble desk and a corner office than I was the day I graduated from college.

When I bought the business, a dusty IBM electric typewriter sat in the corner of the office. Word processors had been introduced but they were still not in common use. I thought, *There must be a way to use that typewriter to make more money.* I expanded the business offerings to include typing services and helped people by editing their written work. I taught my assistant what I knew so she could do it, too. Within six months, I had increased revenues significantly and streamlined the operation, lowering fixed costs.

While I was answering the jangling phones one morning, a well-dressed gentleman came into the office. He was pleasant and warm, and I enjoyed his easy sense of humor. He was patient with the phone calls that kept interrupting our conversation. He became our life and health insurance agent and we became friends. He saw what I was doing to grow the business and told me if I ever wanted to make a change, there was a job waiting for me in his business. I kept thinking about the elegant suits he wore and the Cadillac he drove.

Deregulation of the phone companies was coming, and local phone bills were expected to rise exorbitantly. Equipment, a large expense, would inevitably change. Also, the opportunities for growth were limited; the business had a small geographic area in which I could offer inexpensive service, and I'd worn out a lot of shoe leather going to every business I could find, letting them know about my services.

Don't Be Afraid to Make Changes

I called Rick, our insurance guy, and asked questions about what he did. I thought it would be more exciting and challenging than my little storefront business in a sleepy burg. I sold the business, paid off my father-in-law, took my profits, and ran. I called Rick again and asked him when he wanted me to start. At the same time my marriage was on shaky ground; we had separated and gotten back together with an uneasy truce. I came from a family where there had never been a divorce before, so the D-word was not part of my vocabulary. As inept as I felt about asking for what I wanted in the business world, I was probably worse in my marriage back then.

The life insurance business is challenging. Insurance is known as an "intangible." Nobody wants it, but everyone needs it. I faced customers, married men with children and a wife at home, who literally said, "I don't plan on dying," which blew me away. It was a tough career choice on my marriage since I was away all day and often working very late into the evening. Even so, within three months, I won the Rookie Division of a sales contest put on by an A+ rated national insurance company.

The insurance business requires a massive amount of time to build up a clientele. I saw business clients during the day and personal clients in the evening. It was uncommon for me to arrive home before ten o'clock at night. I realized later I was avoiding the frustration of what waited for me when I got home at night. To compound matters, my husband had plenty of time to find someone newer, younger, and blonder. After five years of a misfit marriage, I was sad but relieved when we parted.

Testosterone-Free Tip: Some women feel that they must put their work ahead of their personal life. Other women say they are serious about their businesses, but if they actually tracked their time and efforts, they would know that their heart is not in their business. Balance is the secret to success. If you are canceling more personal plans than you are keeping, you are out of balance. If your personal life *always* takes precedence over your business life, you may be out of balance, too.

From that inauspicious beginning, I went on to earn more money selling health and life insurance—mostly to small business owners—than I ever thought possible. The truth was that I wasn't doing much selling. My boss was doing most of the selling. I went along on many cases as his sidekick. I burned the midnight oil putting together flawless proposals, crunching numbers, and making him look awesome. He was wowed by my research work. In exchange he gave a big chunk of the commissions to me. But it was his amazing presentations and ability to ask and answer questions that saved the day and closed the sale every time. His genius lay in his clear focus on the customer.

After a couple years, he told me it was time to start running my own accounts. I should have been excited, but instead I was petrified. After all, he was always the front man. He made what he did look easy, but I knew it wasn't. I sucked in a deep breath, opened the Yellow Pages, and started dialing the phone. That was the first terrifying part.

I realize a lot of women would have stopped right there. There were days when I looked for every excuse in the book to avoid getting on the phone. My boss had no magic for me except, "Denise, just do it." Sometimes I would. I would tell myself that I wasn't selling on the phone, just scheduling an appointment.

Walking into a prospective client's office struck fear in my heart. No longer could I stand behind my boss "The Sales Machine." I was so self-conscious I could barely speak. I was positive they would know I was a fraud and an impostor. It was so difficult for me that

I sometimes hoped the person I was supposed to meet would actually forgot about our appointment and be away from the office.

Actually, I had learned the business well; I was apprenticed to the best. But I still had a big problem. When a 28-year-old woman enters the office of middle-aged man who owns a tool and die business (remember, I'm from Detroit), who do you think controls the conversation? If I knew then what I know now, the outcome would've been different. Back then, I felt trivial, small, and scared, and as if I was wasting the client's time. I know now they saw my hesitation and fear, and they often brushed me off in record time. There were many instances when I got back in my car after a meeting, stuck the key in the ignition and burst into tears, feeling like the ultimate failure.

It wasn't much fun anymore.

The odd thing is, I am not shy. You won't find me the wild woman in sequins wearing a lampshade at a party. However, I'm at ease joining a conversation with a group of people, telling jokes, singing if there is music, dancing and having a terrific time. No sweat. In social situations, most people view me as enthusiastic and confident. No one would think in business I felt like a shy little mouse.

Asking for the business struck fear into my heart. Those would-be clients were waiting for me to take the lead and I was too nervous in those days to do anything except follow. I was a woman totally caught up in the male testosterone-heavy version of marketing back then. I did not feel as if I could be myself and I did not know there was another way, either. I needed help, ideas, anything that would help me figure out why I was holding myself back from success. Twenty years before this book was written, I began looking for answers. I have now written the book I needed back then. Thankfully ***Testosterone-Free Marketing*** is here and you do not have to go through the struggle that I experienced. You can just read this book and apply the lessons you discover on these pages.

Summing It Up

§ Over 10 million American women have started businesses in the US alone.

§ Going door-to-door never felt normal; it never felt comfortable. Cold-calling on the phone scared me. And meeting in person was terrifying. That is why I have written this book – so women just like you can market and still be a woman!

§ Balance is a necessary ingredient in all things, especially if you are juggling both a business and a family. Too much of one or the other will only make both flounder. As I learned about balance, I watched my dreams soar. You can, too.

Get Started Now

For the next week, spend five minutes every day writing down what it is about marketing you find frightening, overwhelming or unnerving. Or, write down why you honestly seem to avoid marketing. No one has to see it except you, so be honest. Make a list.

Think of how you might do things differently to transform marketing from being gut-wrenching to fun. If you can find ways to do this, I want to acknowledge you. Maybe you're reading this action step and thinking to yourself, *Is she nuts?* Don't worry. Just do the first half of this action step. As you continue to read, I promise you will start to see marketing as more doable and yes, even fun.

Last Word

For a woman to engage in the testosterone-heavy world can be like going to a gunfight with a pocket knife. There's always another way to prevail.

Chapter Three

We Are Different – Thank Goodness for Small Miracles

"There is no point at which you can say, 'Well, I'm successful now. I might as well take a nap.' "

– Carrie Fisher

I found the world of marketing was made primarily for men. There were many answers to my questions, yet they didn't solve my problems because they didn't answer my concerns as a woman. In fact, the answers were a big part of my problem.

What's Wrong With This Picture?

I started looking for sales training. I went to one seminar after another and discovered sales masters like Tommy Hopkins, Zig Ziglar, and others. I bought their tapes and listened to them over and over. For a little while I felt like someone handed me a golden key. Here were the words. All I needed to do was say the right words, ask the right questions, and I could control the outcome - control my destiny. All I had to do was ask.

But the next time I was in a meeting, something strange happened. The words flew out of my head and I felt as paralyzed as before. Only worse. Something about "The Sales Master's" questions and phrases made me feel uncomfortable. I just could not say those words in front of a customer. Even when I *tried*, I could not force the words from my lips. I wanted to impress clients, but I ended up looking childish. I knew how to help them with their problems, but I couldn't get them to say, "Yes." The closes felt confrontational. As much as I wanted the business, I couldn't do it. I felt like a failure. My short-lived career was slipping. I was 28.

Testosterone-Free Tip: When men teach women testosterone-heavy marketing methods, it's not because they're trying to hold us back. It's because they don't intrinsically get how powerful our femininity is to who we are. When you learn to be attractive (in a marketing sense), customers will want to say "yes" to you. ***Testosterone Free Marketing*** will teach you how to be yourself and get amazing results as you market your business so you can put more cash in your purse. You can do it.

Let's Face It – We're Women

Why couldn't I just say the words the guys in the office told me would work? They wanted me to succeed. They wanted me to win. What was wrong with me? Why couldn't I form the words and overcome the customer's objections and "nail the sale"?

The problem was that I was a woman and it was men who developed those sales tactics. They were made for someone whose body, psyche, and personality were fundamentally different from mine. Marketing has always been a man's business. Let's face it: just one generation ago almost all businesses were men's businesses. While woman have entered the corporate world in droves, banging on the glass ceilings to knock on the door of senior management, the world of marketing hasn't kept pace. Many still see it as a "dog-eat-dog, go for the jugular" world. "Overcome those objections and nail that sale." That's what the seasoned pros said.

The goal was to find ways to make the customer uncomfortable by reminding them of a problem they may not realize they have. My job was to make them so uncomfortable that when I provided the solution, they would say yes and write a check. To me it felt wrong. Don't most people understand their problems and issues better than anyone? It seemed manipulative. I didn't want to be pushy; I wanted to be a friend. But there were no selling tools to help me. I felt as if I was standing naked with all my lumps and bumps exposed for all to see. I bumbled along.

Like effective marketing, good selling is about building rapport and solving customers' problems. But at the end of the day, it was still about "slamming 'em to the mat" again and again. That strategy didn't work for me and yet I didn't know any alternatives. I could not find a single book about marketing meant to help the millions of women who were entering the workforce and starting their own businesses.

The Language of Marketing Is the Language of Men

Selling has a language all its own. “He hit a home run!” the boss says when someone lands a new account. “It’s time to get back in the game,” he says to a salesperson whose numbers have lagged. “Use all the weapons in your arsenal,” he says in a high-pressure situation with a deadline looming. The vernacular of marketing has always been masculine and aggressive. “Go for the jugular” and “Clobber the competition” have withstood the test of time.

But do these phrases help us feel like who we are? We’re women. We create and give birth to the human race. We nurture our children, our lovers, our parents, and our friends. We look for connection not competition. There is a reason why combat duty doesn’t suit most of us - both on the battlefield and in the boardroom. We don’t want our business to be a war. We want everyone to win. Men elbow each other, and put another notch on their belt. It’s about keeping score. Women build friendships, nurture our families and look for ways to help others. Our “wins” don’t have a beginning, middle or end. They flow happily along the continuum of life.

Does winning have a gender? On the surface it would appear that men tote up more outwardly impressive results. Their results are measurable: units sold, deals closed, and profit margins. Women’s results are less precise. What is the value of a loving relationship, a friend, or a happy child? These are the victories we have sought. I love when someone says, “Yes, I want to do business with you,” but the victory would feel hollow if I lied or was pushy to my customer. If that’s true for you, then you will breathe a sigh of relief as you discover the secrets of *“Testosterone Free Marketing.”*

“Business has no gender,” one woman said angrily. Ah, but people do. Our gender is a deep part of who we are. We are people first and women second. A close second.

Business Ownership Levels the Playing Field

Owning a small business is a world with few road maps oriented toward us and our needs as women. However, one thing I enjoy about entrepreneurship is that the playing field is more level.

- § The person who's best for the job gets the business as long as they market well.
- § People do business with people they like.
- § There is virtually no office politics. There can be community "politics" or industry "politics" but it's not usually from the person across the hall.
- § Say goodbye to the glass ceiling.
- § You do not have to compete against others. Be your best and most unique version of you.

Small business owners tend to have maverick personalities and so gender is often less of a consideration in who they use to provide products and services. Can you get the job done? Do I enjoy doing business with you? These are important questions. No one is clawing for the corner office. Even competing businesses in the same industry often seek to find a truce. It's an easier way to live. But you still have to ask for the business. You still must be a leader.

In January of 1992, I moved from Detroit to San Diego. Most of my family had left Michigan and I felt no reason to stay. I wanted people to be impressed with me, yet it earned me a reputation among other women as "bitchy." And in business meetings I was not impressive, I was terrified. I wanted to relax. I decided to surround myself only with people who accepted me as me. That meant I had to figure out who that was.

I started attending networking meetings. There were lots of women starting small businesses. I got busy writing freelance advertising copy, brochures, and marketing plans for other small business owners. I experienced lots of fits and starts. I wanted to know more about myself. I wanted to know more about others. Mostly, I wanted to feel more comfortable in my own skin—something I had never felt before.

I grew. I started telling the truth rather than what I thought people wanted to hear. I gave up my quest to "be impressive" and decided what was more important was to be authentic. I abandoned the marble desk and corner office fantasy. I decided that was more about my parents wish for me to be secure than anything that mattered to me. I liked working with small business owners. It suited me. When I started, my office was in the small, spare bedroom of my two-bedroom cottage.

One sun-dappled spring afternoon, I was walking the stone paved path to my mailbox. I looked forward to these little breaks. I would meet my next-door neighbor on my way. He was a home-based business owner as well, and we would stop and chat for a few minutes before going back to work.

Something clicked in my head that afternoon. I suddenly realized people didn't care about me. Oh sure, I had nice friends who liked me and wanted me to be happy. But in a marketing sense, people just didn't care. All that time I'd spent trying to "be impressive" was wasted because it was much more important that they wanted me to think *they* were impressive.

It was a pivotal moment. I didn't have to worry about impressing them; they were too busy trying to impress me. They cared more about their life then they would ever care about mine. My past "failures" didn't matter. I felt free. In fact it actually became one of my rules of marketing: Stop spending so much time trying to impress others and instead spend your energy being impressed with them. (To find out more about my marketing rules go to http://www.MarketingforHer.com and click on "Keyword Search" and then "Denise's Marketing Rules.")

I didn't read a book and become The Overnight Amazing Marketing Babe. I had spent years feeling painfully uncomfortable. Nothing helped me deal with my uncomfortable feelings and reactions. Change didn't happen instantly. I had to figure out why I was so distressed in marketing and selling situations. Years later I started talking with other women and learned I wasn't alone. It became my passion to answer these questions to help me and other women. Gradually I felt comfortable and at ease selling and marketing. Now marketing and selling is fun and I make more money than ever.

Transform Your Thinking, Transform Your Life

Finally I discovered the key to getting people to buy my products, services and ideas. Those closing questions, designed to back people into a corner and convince them they had a problem only I could solve, were unnecessary. They didn't need me dredging up new problems. I just had to accept people as they were and help them talk about and solve the problems they already had.

Since then, my life has transformed. My income has multiplied again and again. I am me, with all my flaws, my intelligence and my sense of humor. I share the things that make me feel good and the things that scare the wits out of me. I am regarded by many as a marketing expert, and get compliments that are embarrassing to repeat. I get standing ovations when I speak. I have helped people galvanize their resources and make a big chunk of money in a short period of time.

As this metamorphosis occurred, I decided my mission was supporting people in going for their dreams. That's why I love working with small and home-based business owners. I support people in going for their dreams and visions by sharing marketing strategies and knowledge. I also constantly meet women who are excited about their business but are as terrified about marketing it as I was. I also love encouraging those women who want to close the door on that corporate office and finally control their own destiny.

Chances are you will see yourself over and over again in this book. You will recognize patterns and meet other women who share your concerns. At the end of each chapter, you will find action steps under the heading "Get Started Now" that will help you change how you think about marketing and market with less effort, more fun and better results. This book can help you change your life. Taking action on what you learn will help you create more cash flow in less time and with more ease. You will develop confidence. You will understand marketing and enjoy a lot more money and freedom as a result.

Testosterone-Free Tip: It is not necessary to work nonstop to achieve success. Schedule time throughout the day and the week to take small breaks. Get out for coffee or lunch with a friend or acquaintance at least once a week. As a home-based business owner, it's easy to become isolated. Women especially need the friendship and support of others. It picks us up and gives us the support and the motivation to solve problems. Besides, networking is a wonderful way to make new contacts and customers. Consciously choose friends who are uplifting and supportive.

I do ***Testosterone Free Marketing*** teleclasses with women as a much more personal way than this book to help them to grow. They journey through a process of self-growth and consequently business growth, and I support them to create more cash flow. To be successful you cannot separate your business from your mindset and what you bring to the table. (To discover more go to www.MarketingforHer.com click on "Products" and then click on "Teleclass.")

Don't just skim this book. Read it more than once. It's your book. Make notes and observations. Keep a journal. Complete the action steps. Write your Letter of Commitment and sign and date it. Treat this as if your business depended on it, because it does. I'm rooting for you.

Get Started Now

Are You a "Yin" or "Yang" Marketer?

The terms "Yin" and "Yang" are discussed in greater detail in Chapters Eight and Nine. For this quiz you can use a quick definition. "Yin" refers to qualities that are feminine. "Yang" refers to qualities that are masculine. The Yin and Yang are represented by the Chinese symbol with a circle containing two swirls within that almost look like tadpoles curled cozily together. Yin and Yang can be applied to many things and when someone says something is "Yang," it's like saying, "It's a 'guy' thing." You see the ancient Yin-Yang symbol in front of each "Testosterone-Free Tip" throughout this book

Use a check mark or an X to indicate whether each statement below seems "true" or "false" for you:

1. I want to improve my marketing skills but I'm not sure where to start. Learning about marketing and actually doing it seem to be two very different things.

2. I enjoy selling my product or service in person. The challenge of sales and helping customers say "yes" is always fun for me.

3. I put a lot of effort in making sure my office space reflects my style. I've decorated it to make me and my customers/clients feel at home.

4. I personally contact new leads and people I've recently met every week. I'm comfortable telling them about my product or service and asking them to buy.

5. I worked hard to develop a great logo and put much thought into creating attractive business cards that reflect me, my style and what my business is about.

6. I have a great elevator speech I use in networking situations. I'm at ease sharing who I am and how I can help others.

7. I work hard researching my product or industry so I can answer any questions that might possibly come up. I feel I can never know enough.

8. I love the thrill of competition and I'm pretty ambitious about winning in business and in other aspects of my life.

9. I know I do a great job. I'm looking forward to the day when others will finally notice and recognize how great my product/service truly is.

10. I thrive on new situations where I am in the public eye. I love getting out there, talking with people and taking chances even if I'm not always prepared.

All people contain elements of both masculine and feminine. The odd-numbered statements are Yin or typically feminine ways of thinking and acting. These are things we may do when we act from our feminine selves. The even numbered statements are Yang or typically masculine ways of thinking and acting. If you answered "false" to more of the Yang statements – you are like millions of women around the world.

Summing It Up

§ If "putting yourself out there" does not feel natural, you are about normal. The "testosterone heavy" sales and marketing methods won't help you overcome your concerns. They ignore the fact that you're a woman.

§ Celebrate each new client or customer with a small reward. Be patient with yourself and look for gradual shifts, not instant gratification.

§ The questions and closes I was taught were confrontational and made me feel awful. Thousands of women business owners I've coached feel the same.

§ Marketing has always been one of the most masculine activities in business

§ We are people first and women second. A close second.

§ When you're in business for yourself there is no glass ceiling but there are no mentors either. People do business with people they like.

§ You must market consistently to have a viable business.

Last Word:

In the long run, cooperation rather than competition will bring you more clients and make for a more harmonious life all round.

Chapter Four

Believe in Yourself and Your Vision

"In every aspect of our lives, we are always asking ourselves,
How am I of value? What is my worth?
Yet I believe that worthiness is our birthright."

— Oprah Winfrey

Bethany was a weight loss success story. Ten years ago she lost fifty pounds. Unlike most of the population, she was diligent, kept the weight off and developed a sleek, sexy body. She became a personal trainer and got a degree in exercise physiology. She was a fountain of wisdom on the subjects of health, nutrition, and fitness. Blonde, slim, with blue eyes and a dazzling smile, men were drawn to her wherever she went. At 37 she looked like 23. Bethany had a dream to write a diet book for women and conduct seminars to share her secrets, but she knew she would enter a crowded market full of celebrities and fads.

She agonized for months about the title of her book. As her coach, when I gave her a "homework" assignment, she would complete half of it before our next coaching call. Before inching forward, she wanted more re-assurance and feedback that she was on track with her idea.

Testosterone-Free Tip: Polling everyone before making a decision will only cause you more agony and uncertainty. Testing is worthwhile but there comes a time when it is necessary to take the plunge. Balance is the key to success.

It was easy to see Bethany lacked confidence. Her posture was slumped all the time. Her comments were couched as questions, looking for approval. I kept working with her because no matter how halting her progress, she still was moving forward. She wasn't yet creating the momentum needed to really succeed, but she kept trying.

The Psyche of a Millionaire

I have worked with five millionaires. Every self-made millionaire I've ever met possessed abundant self-confidence. They ask for what they want. They have the confidence to communicate why their product or service is better. They step out boldly, know their value, and ask for what they're worth. This confidence is almost spiritually based. It is seeing the God or a Higher Power within and knowing they are a reflection of that wisdom and grace.

On the other hand, the media and the Hollywood image machine churn out the stereotype of wealthy people as greedy, lying, cheating, soulless, self-centered, chomping on a big cigar, and devoid of human warmth. This is, by far, the exception and not the rule.

One day Bethany decided to take a bold step. She screwed up her courage and talked to the owner of the gym where she worked. She told him she wanted to conduct a weight loss workshop. Her plan was to charge a small amount for the three-hour event. Then she would offer a teleseminar. (A teleseminar is a class presented on a bridge phone line, and participants call from home and listen to the instructor live on the phone.) With my help, Bethany made a flyer, including her dramatic before and after pictures. She started talking to people she worked out with at the gym. Women started signing up.

Put Your Focus Where It Belongs

One week before her workshop, a panic-stricken Bethany called me, "Denise, I want to do this, but I'm worried. What if someone asks a question I can't answer? What if I look like a fool? What if people think I'm a phony?" The truth bubbled to the surface. Bethany lacked self-confidence, and she needed to either get over it or call off the workshop.

I asked Bethany to envision a group of people at a party. Some are outgoing, others are listeners, and one person is shy. I asked her to imagine she was the shy person. "As the shy person, what are you thinking about?" I asked.

"Lets see," she sighed, "I'm thinking …"

- Do my clothes look okay?
- Are people talking about me?
- I'm having a bad hair day.
- I don't want people to think I'm eating like a pig.
- If I say something, people might think I'm stupid.

- I wonder if that cute guy thinks I'm attractive?
- I don't fit in. Why did they invite me?

"How can a shy person listen to a conversation or make a new friend if she's constantly worried about me, me, me?" I asked Bethany.

"She's worried about how other people respond to her," she said.

"Same thing. You are not taking a genuine interest in anyone. You're totally focused on you. You need to put your focus where it belongs. You're not asking questions or making eye contact." I assured her I'd never met a millionaire who had problems making eye contact. "If you noticed this shy person, what would you think?"

"I would think she was self-absorbed. Stuck-up, in fact," said Bethany.

Being self-conscious and shy is actually selfish behavior. You're unable to take an interest in other people; because you can't stop thinking about yourself. "This seminar is not about you, Bethany," I said.

"It's not?" she asked.

"No. It's for the women who pay to attend. You're just there to help them."

"Oh, of course," she said, her voice brightening.

If you are present for the customers you are serving, and if you care about them, they will pick up on your caring energy. Caring is one of our strengths as women. I gave one of my best workshops when I was sick with the flu and losing my voice, but because I was passionate, it came across. They didn't care about my froggy voice or my cough. What matters is your joy, passion and concern about helping people.

If you're fully present with the people you intend to serve, they don't care if:

- Your clothes aren't perfect.
- You cannot answer every question immediately.
- You're having a bad hair day.
- You say something a little silly…

And…

- Everyone will find you "attractive" because your energy is infectious.
- You will always fit in.

"So I shouldn't worry if I feel stupid or dorky?" Bethany asked.

"Blow it off and move on," I answered. "Make a joke of it at your expense. Laugh. It will put everyone else at ease."

Several years ago I was given an award, presented in front of a room of 400 people. Most of those people knew me. As I jogged to the stage, I tripped and fell on my way up the stairs to the stage. All I could think about was 400 people staring at my big butt. You could hear a pin drop. The president of the company winced. I sprang to my feet, took the microphone, and said, "The only thing I bruised was my ego." He laughed. The audience laughed. It was over. Later, not a single person said anything mean-spirited. When I spoke the next day, the room was packed and I received a standing ovation.

Two weeks later, I got an email from Bethany. Her first workshop was a success. The room was packed. Feeling scared and self-conscious was the last thing on her mind. She had fun. Forty percent of the attendees purchased her teleseminar. She made almost $3,000 from that Saturday morning workshop, and was elated.

Bethany broke through her fear to a new level of confidence. With her newfound courage, and my help, she started writing a book proposal. She self-published her book and continues to take strides forward.

Every self-made wealthy person I've ever met has one thing in common—self-confidence. Bethany had to increase her confidence to accomplish her dreams.

Your "Who Am I?" Questions

It should come as no surprise that many women suffer from a lack of self-confidence. We spend our lives nurturing others while neglecting ourselves. It's a breeze to build others up and tell them how fabulous they are. We support others, encourage them and say, "You go, girl!" But we won't say it for ourselves. When asked why, women often say, "I'm just being honest."

That's not true. We all have gifts to share. We have experienced triumph and tragedy. What do you have to share with the world? How are you different or special?

Right now, sit down and create five short lists. These are your "Who Am I" questions. Jot down each of the following titles on a separate sheet of paper, and then ask yourself:

- What do I like about me?
- What do others like about me?
- What do I do well?
- What do I enjoy doing most?
- What positive characteristics do people see in me when we first meet?

Write through the heart of someone who loves you exactly as you are. Are you outgoing? Are you compassionate, wise and a good listener? Do you possess the gift of making others feel special? Write until you can think of no more. Take a deep breath. By writing the answers to these five questions you will start seeing yourself in a different light. When you complete each list, you will discover amazing things about you.

On the surface, this appears to be a personal growth exercise. It's also the foundation of who you are as "a product" to be marketed. People will do business with you because of you, not your product. They can probably get your product and even your service elsewhere. What are the qualities you provide on your five lists that could be included in your marketing message to make you more attractive? This forms the basis of your marketing message.

Self-confidence Is an Inside Job

With all the emphasis on self-esteem since the 1980s and all the changes women have undergone, you might think that young women would have much better self-esteem and self-confidence than middle-aged and older women. Surprisingly, it's not true. Even though parenting skills have eliminated spanking and added tools to help children grow up with greater self-esteem, it doesn't always turn out that way. Even if a child is told over and over again that she is wonderful and adorable, if she watched parents who had low or poor self-esteem, she will struggle. If the "role models" she grew up around were of people who did not possess confidence and self-esteem, she will not possess it herself. She will come across as confident on the outside but may still feel fearful on the inside. These mixed messages create confusion and women who wonder why they are so outgoing in some situations yet so anxious or hesitant in other situations.

Once I treated a friend to lunch and said, "I'm about to take on a big project and I need all the confidence I can get. What do you see as my positive qualities?" I listened and returned the gift. I was looking for positive feedback from the outside rather than looking for ways to develop confidence within. Looking for self-worth from outside yourself will turn you into a "self-acceptance junkie." True self-confidence comes from within.

How do you develop a core of confidence when it seems the world is eager to tear you down? Here's a secret question I ask women when their confidence is lagging: "Do you believe in God, a Higher Power, Buddha, Allah or Jehovah?"

Whether you're Jewish, Christian, Buddhist, Muslim, Hindu, or whatever, all the world's major religions share a few basic tenets. Over 80 percent of Americans believe in God or a Higher Power, and have either a strong core of non-religious spirituality or a religious affiliation. If you are among them, this little exercise will help you.

If you believe in God or a Higher Power, chances are, you understand it as a presence, an energy, a knowingness that resides within you. It's a part of who you are as a person. Most people agree that our Higher Power is the source of our intelligence, wisdom, and creative solutions. But they do not always make the cause-and-effect leap from that Higher Power within to tapping into it when they need a source of confidence and wisdom. If we listen and pay attention, we can tap into that higher source of wisdom, intelligence and creativity any time we choose. All we must do is remember to ask and listen.

When I remember to ask God for answers, I always get the right ones. I don't always like the answers, but they are infallibly the right ones. Then I have a choice. I can act on those answers … or not. When I need to feel confident or make good decisions, I tap into that infinite source of wisdom and creativity. That source makes me feel more confident, not in a swaggering, bragging way, but in a quiet, deep way seen and felt by others.

It can do the same for you if you ask and listen. You do not have to be different or act like someone you are not. You are perfect exactly as you are. You have only to remember to listen to that still, small voice and heed its wisdom. If you haven't listened in a long time, it may take a while before the voice of your intuition becomes clear. Be patient. It's there. Just listen.

A Stronger, More Confident You

Have you ever heard of "fake it till you make it"? It works. I just wish it wasn't so "fake." A self-made millionaire friend of mine once suggested instead that I "practice the future." I can't tell you how many times I've used this strategy when I had to project confidence and I felt rotten. Men do this all the time. They exude confidence and conviction because they are conditioned to do so.

Have you ever wondered how men can display so much confidence?" While we try to get every detail perfect behind the scenes, they walk through the door and their energy, their larger-than-life presence takes over. How do they do it? The answer: They make it up as they go along. They jump off a cliff and build a parachute on the way down. We don't need to be like men, but we can learn from them.

How would a stronger, more confident you act? You would not:

- Giggle nervously.
- Apologize before sharing your opinion.
- Babble to fill the silence.

- Allow others to interrupt you or cut you off by saying, "Excuse me, may I finish my point."
- Speak in a soft tone when you want to make an important point.
- Talk about your dreams as not just "a silly dream" but with seriousness and passion as if they were real plans.
- Look down your nose at anyone.
- Wear jewelry that jangles or makeup that is harsh.
- Touch your face or hair.
- Take copious notes like a secretary.

Instead, you would:

- Use body language comfortably, with occasional wide-sweeping gestures.
- Make your point in a way that's succinct, using powerful language.
- Laugh heartily when it's appropriate.
- Break a talk or presentation into chunks you can memorize.
- Take questions at the end.
- Speak with energy, enthusiasm and verve.
- Shake hands firmly.
- Smile from time to time.
- Wear clothes that express your style, but that are appropriate.
- Say, "I'll get you an answer by tomorrow" if you don't know the answer immediately.

- Warmly say, "That's interesting but it's not why we're here today," when someone goes off on a tangent.
- Sit back comfortably in your chair occasionally rather than leaning forward as if you're desperate for approval or acceptance.

Testosterone-Free Tip: Shake hands with confidence. The inside web of skin between your thumb and index finger should meet the inside web of the other person's thumb and index finger. Shake firmly and don't crush. "Dead-fish handshakes" are a no-no. Shake until you see the color of the other person's eyes.

When you "fake it till you make it" or "practice the future," you're never faking or practicing for too long. Chances are, in a few minutes, you will begin to feel more self-confident. When your inner confidence matches your outer image, it spells "confidence." You are rich in creativity, wisdom, and inner beauty. (To learn more about developing self-confidence go to www.MarketingforHer.com, click on "Keyword Search" and then click on "Unshakeable Self-Confidence.")

Take One Step Backward First

There is no defeat until you give up. You always have options. Perhaps you need to consider new, creative options that seem out of the box, with the brainstorming help of others who are positive and supportive. You may have to take a step backward first before taking three steps forward. Your confidence and positive energy will draw people to you even if it feels as if you're faking or practicing at first.

Step into your power. Three lines of the famous poem "Desiderata" state:

"You are a child of the universe
no less than the trees and the stars;
you have a right to be here."

Summing It Up

- § Successful people possess abundant self-confidence.
- § Even if your parents tried to raise you with self-esteem, if their behavior was that of a person who lacked confidence, you may have picked up mixed messages.
- § When you look outside for the source of your self-confidence, you'll never get enough. Genuine self-confidence comes from within.
- § Entrepreneurs only do business with people they like and most people love others who possess a positive point of view.
- § Even if you fake it till you make it, if you take action, you will start developing unshakeable self-confidence.
- § If you are fully present for customers you serve, and you care about them, they will pick up your caring energy. They will not care if you are not perfect.
- § If you believe in a Higher Power, you understand *it* is the source of all intelligence, wisdom, and creative solutions.
- § When your positive inner feelings about you match your outer image, that combination spells "self-confidence."

Get Started Now

* Do the five-list exercise above. Write until you can think of no more. Then write at least two more items before moving on to the next list.

* Make a list of people who could help you. Write down everyone who could possibly help, even if you have no idea how to contact them or even if you believe they are "too famous," "too wealthy" or "too anything."

* Once you have the list, brainstorm with friends and colleagues about ways you could possibly meet them so they can mentor you.

Last Word:

Winning isn't just about *getting* new clients and business but about *keeping* them, year in, year out, which means that your relationship is about *them*, not you. So nurture them.

Chapter Five

Courage, Like Love, Comes Straight from the Heart

"A good woman is like a tea bag. You never know how strong she is until you get her in hot water."

— Eleanor Roosevelt

Getting started takes courage. It's easier to linger at the starting line, wishing your dreams would come true. The "monster" that holds you back from starting is fear—fear of failure, fear of looking stupid, fear of not fitting in, fear of rejection. Fear holds many women back, doing brings success. Your power to love can help you find the answers to your marketing challenges and fears.

What would you do if you discovered an email in your inbox like this?

> What can I do about my fear? I'm so afraid I can barely move. I have six children and I'm getting laid off from my job as a nurse. My husband has been on disability for three years. He seems incapable of dealing with our finances and has given up that responsibility completely. I just found out he hasn't paid a bill in over two months. It's all on my shoulders. There is a growing pile of bills on my desk I am afraid to open. I'm so scared. What should I do? - Caroline

This email landed in my inbox three days after my boss left on a 22-city book tour. All his emails were forwarded to me. His travel schedule would be far too demanding to answer the daily deluge of email.

What would you tell Caroline? Telling her to calm down and be rational would only make matters worse. Sounds like the advice a lot of our husbands and partners would give, doesn't it? It's not bad, but it's not very helpful or reassuring either.

Your Strength as a Woman Is Part of Your Core

Instead, I told Caroline the opposite: "Pick a time when you're alone at home. Get rid of your kids and husband for an hour or two if you must. Look at that pile of bills. Dump them on the kitchen table. Stamp your feet, scream, and throw pillows around. Have a good cry about how unfair it is. Get it out of your system. Then take a few deep breaths, sit down, and start opening those bills. Go through everything one-by-one."

She did. Caroline stomped around the house, yelling, slamming doors and crying until she collapsed on her bed in giggles, her face wet with tears. Then she opened the bills. It wasn't pretty, but at least she knew the facts. I've heard men refer to our feminine tears as "breaking down," while we think of it as "cleansing" and "getting it out of our system."

Caroline crafted a plan, not just to pay the bills, but to never have to worry like this again. She was fortunate. Caroline had a supportive family. She went to a family member who lent her enough money to cover the bills and support her family for a few months. At the time she wrote me, she had attended a seminar on real estate investing a few months previously. Now she had a little capital. She bought a couple pieces of investment real estate for closing costs. The mortgage was being paid by renters and she had positive cash flow at the end of each month. She bought a couple more properties. Her monthly cash flow increased. It flowed in, slowly at first. She discovered within herself the courage, confidence and qualities of a winner to pull herself up and help her family.

Caroline began paying her relative back. When he started getting checks in the mail after just a few months, he asked her what she was doing. She told him about her real estate purchases. "I wish I could pay you faster, but that would take more up-front money," she laughed.

"How much more?" he asked. They came to an agreement and he wrote her another check. Now they're business partners.

This story is an example of a woman who transformed her fear. She turned it into courage and gradually become profitable and successful. She did it, not by being rational, but by going a little crazy for a few minutes. Then she asked for help. She admitted to me that until the debts were paid off in full, she went berserk a few more times.

Courage Is Not Just a "Guy Thing"

The root of the word courage comes from the French *coeur*, which means "heart." To have courage means to put your heart first into what you do. You should also use your wisdom when it comes to making decisions. But the first urging must be from your heart.

I love visiting art museums. When I travel to a new city, I enjoy spending a relaxing afternoon enjoying old masterpieces. I've been to many major art museums in the U.S. and the Louvre and Giverny in Paris, Topkapi in Istanbul and others.

Some Renaissance era paintings depict battle scenes. If you look closely, you see faces filled with fear and courage. I used to believe courage meant having no fear. I now know that courage has nothing to do with being fearless. Courage is about moving beyond what you feel and doing the thing you fear most, so you grow emotionally, spiritually or financially. Every time we take a new risk, we become uncomfortable. Maybe your palms sweat or your heart races. Maybe you wonder if the time you invest will be worth it.

In the book, *Feel the Fear and Do It Anyway*, author Susan Jeffers says fear can be broken into three levels: (1) the surface story, that is, what we tell ourselves and others; (2) things that "happen," an accident or the loss of a loved one, and; (3) things that require action such as changing careers, buying a property or starting a business.

If we let it, fear can permeate our lives. Level One fears are situations in which we are openly fearful. These can be reasonable fears. Level One fears might include fear of fire, falling off a tall building, or drowning if you're not a good swimmer. We can get over many Level One fears but sometimes they are reasonable. Jeffers says Level Two fears have to do with our inner state of mind. How do you feel about an action you're thinking about taking? How will it change your life? Level Three fears are about getting down to the nitty-gritty. Are you ready? Will you take action? It boils down to, "I'm afraid I can't handle it!" Jeffers says, every time you feel afraid to make a conscious, positive change, remind yourself it's because you don't feel good about yourself.

Long-lasting confidence comes not as much from repeating affirmations over and over, but from doing good, courageous things for yourself and others. It comes from taking a chance and action. In business, courage is about being pro-active.

There are moments when each of us reaches a crossroads. Brenda had the finest education money could buy, but financially she felt her life was a big, fat zero. Brenda had a hunch about a marketing strategy she wanted to try. Fear held her back. If she had just moved forward, she would have gotten a lot of visibility and new clients. Brenda was so upset with herself for not acting that her stomach was in knots.

The source of her fear was her mother. Overprotective and afraid of her own shadow, the fears she projected onto her daughter still controlled her. Brenda achieved academically and also became licensed as a master scuba-diver, not a sport for the faint of heart. What held her back? It doesn't matter. By responding with conscious choices instead of knee-jerk reactions, you can make positive changes and act with more courage and confidence.

Many people discover that when they put their fear under a magnifying glass, the gray cloud that's held them back for years is baseless. It has no more substance than air. It's an annoying fog that has obscured their vision and prevented them from seeing clearly.

Fear Is the Opposite of Love

Fear rejects new ideas. Fear discriminates and prejudges people unfairly. Fear is the opposite of love. Fear stops growth dead in its tracks; love hastens our growth emotionally, spiritually, and financially.

I responded to Brenda with the following email: "Just because your mom was a certain way doesn't mean you have to be that way, too. You can choose differently. Search your heart. Your concern around losing money comes from a belief that supports fear more than growth. Fear permeates everything if you let it. You have developed a belief that if you succeed, something awful will happen. What do you deserve?"

You don't have to spend years of therapy to realize your fears are not serving you. You don't have to unwind the tangled web of how a family member influenced you. You can choose another strategy. What would you do if people couldn't control you? Think of all the energy people pour into trying to control others to keep things "safe." If a family member can no longer control you, you may have to re-define your relationship. If that person is negative, you may choose to phase that person out of your life or limit your exposure to their negativity.

There are people who simply are not happy unless they are controlling others. You can say, "I love you, Mom (or Dad or whoever), but I'm choosing differently." When you choose a different way of responding, the person who has been trying to control you may get upset with you for a time. When you stop giving your power away to others, the balance in the relationship shifts significantly. You can choose not to get caught up in the drama. You don't have to react; you can choose to respond. You're an adult now.

Jeffers says, "Every time you encounter something that forces you to 'handle it,' your self-esteem is raised. You learn to trust that you will survive no matter what happens. And in this way your fears are diminished immeasurably."

It's true. Our comfort zone expands to embrace our new behavior. Once you do what made you fearful, it's no longer the stuff of sleepless nights. Have you ever sent a sales letter to thousands of people, gone on a local talk radio show as a guest or spoken onstage in front of hundreds of people? When you take that step, there is a point of no return. If you feel it's the right thing to do but fear is holding you back, then it's time to take action. (To learn more about taking action in the face of your fear, go to www.MarketingForHer.com, click on "Keyword Search" and then "Courage in Motion" and also "Emotional Freedom.")

Outside Your Comfort Zone

Working for a person who demands excellence is not a picnic. Robert G. Allen, the mega bestselling author and my former boss, was the most fair, even-keeled person I'd ever met. He would kid and joke with me, though he had a serious side, too. Why is working for someone at the top challenging? They are driven to excel. So, they push others to excel the way they push themselves.

When I first started working for him, he'd give me a task and I'd reply, "Gee, Bob, I've never done that before". He'd look up and say with a smile, "Well, figure it out, Denise." It reminded me of how my Dad would challenge me to do the math homework I hated. It forced me to expand my comfort zone.

Most of us tend to ignore the things that we don't enjoy doing. I love writing, I love being around people. I'm passionate about marketing. But I realize there are things I hate doing. For example,

I hate dealing with "I can't" people. They almost always say "no." Technical glitches are the biggest thing I hate. I would rather gouge out my eyeballs then talk with "Tech Support" on the phone. I would rather pack a cell phone back in its box and return it rather than figure out why it won't work. I hate doing things that require a lot of detail and methodical work, such as filling out forms and bookkeeping. I used to avoid these tasks but now I realize it's critical that I at least be willing to save all my receipts and turn them over to a bookkeeper to sort them out. It's part of owning a business so I do it.

These annoyances were a mask for fears I was unwilling to acknowledge. They were my black cloud. Sometimes we have to be like Caroline, the woman facing months of unpaid bills at the beginning of this chapter, and go nuts for a few minutes and then calm down and solve the problem. If you wait until you feel supremely confident before doing anything new, you'll never start. Of all the items on your to-do list, move the things that make you nervous to the top of your list. The rest of the day will be easier.

As you start taking action on the *Testosterone Free Marketing* strategies that follow, you will be faced with new decisions. It's normal to be uncomfortable when this happens. Fear is not an indicator you are doing the wrong thing. Your fear is an indicator that you are facing something new. You are growing beyond your old boundaries.

You have the power to create what you want, starting now. Start by changing your vocabulary. Instead of saying "I can't," say "I won't." Instead of saying "I can," say "I will." Take responsibility for your choices. Small shifts in language move you out of being a *victim* and into being a *victor*. You may still feel afraid, but you are taking positive action.

See Every Experience as a Lesson

It's common for people to feel regret when they finally understand how much time they have wasted being disappointed and afraid. Once they see how their thoughts have resulted in a lack of courage, they see their comfort zone gradually become smaller and more limited. Many times I've heard people say, "Oh, to only have back all those years." Everything is a learning experience, especially when you own your own business. When we understand that we have a choice in how we respond to our circumstances, life's sad moments become less significant. We no longer experience dramatic "lessons," and life and our businesses become joyful and successful. (To learn more about courage, go to www.MarketingforHer.com, click on "Keyword Search" and then on "Getting Unstuck.")

In his book *Risking,* Dr. David Viscott said, "The time you spent suffering was not wasted if it provided a point of resolution for you. Merely being able to say, 'I will never go back to that life again,' can be a source of strength for maintaining a commitment to change."

Summing It Up

§ When you take positive action and move energy, good things will happen.

§ Fear is the opposite of love. Fear will hold you back; love can transform fear into courage and get you past many hurdles.

§ Stop thinking about all the ways a marketing strategy won't work and starting looking for the ways that it will work.

§ When you pre-judge people and ideas, you miss out on benefiting from the ways they may be able to help you and your business.

§ Fear stops growth dead in its tracks. Personal growth and business growth are closely aligned. Moving forward in the face of your fears is courage.

§ Do the thing you fear. Building a successful business is about moving energy and creating something real out of thin air.

Get Started Now

If you are committed to positive change, you can develop a courageous response to fear. Go back and read your Letter of Commitment from Chapter One again and then take the following action steps:

- Focus on the action you want to take but have been afraid to attempt.
- Identify the sources of your fear, but don't dwell on this. Some people get stuck here forever.
- Turn down this voice like turning down the volume on a radio. Turn it way down so that it is barely a whisper.
- Now, focus on the voices that are the opposite of your fear. Positive voices. Let them become powerful in your mind. Turn these voices way up, like the volume on a radio. Listen to the voice that says, "Go for it!" and "You can do it!" Visualize yourself successful and getting the results you want. What does that feel like?
- Repeat this process until you hear supportive enthusiastic messages in a clear, compelling voice.

- Take the action you feared. Call customers who have been on the fence. Tell them that you believe it would be in their best interest to move forward and do business with you. Write that sales letter and send it to everyone on your list. Accept that speaking engagement. Go ahead, do it!

- Consider joining a MasterMind group. The purpose of a MasterMind group is to have other people believe in you and support you in your goals on a weekly basis.

  (To learn more about MasterMinding go to:

  http://www.MarketingforHer.com, click on "Keyword Search" and then "MasterMinding.")

Keeping a Daily Journal will help you focus and re-frame your thoughts as you face your fears. Once your thoughts, feelings, and beliefs are written in front of you, it is easier to be more objective with what is going on inside.

Here are some questions to get you started.

- What am I afraid of right now?
- What am I trying to avoid?
- If I wasn't afraid, what would I do differently?
- What do I fear other people might think of me?
- What would I have to change to be courageous?
- What's the worst that could happen?
- And if that happens, then what?

When we face our fears, we sometimes realize how silly they truly are.

Last Word:

Ships are safe while in harbor, but they are built for sailing on the open seas.

Chapter Six

Getting Out of "Overwhelm" Forever

"As we drive along this road called life, occasionally a gal will find herself a little lost. And when that happens, I guess she has to let go of the coulda, shoulda, woulda, buckle up and just ***keep going.****"*

— Sarah Jessica Parker

One fear I hear from women more than men is the fear of feeling overwhelmed. Overwhelm happens when you have too much to do and don't know what to do next. It is like driving down the freeway and slamming on the brakes with your left foot while your right foot is firmly on the accelerator. This chapter will help you discover why you may be prone to feeling overwhelmed. More importantly, you will learn techniques to keep "overwhelm" at bay while maintaining your momentum.

Fear Disguised as Overwhelm

We wear so many different hats. Mother. Wife. Daughter. Employee or business owner. Each one is demanding. We support and nurture the people we love. Even if your husband or partner is the greatest person in the world, chances are, day in and day out, you provide more emotional support than anyone in your home.

Men tend to say to me, "Denise, I have all these choices. I'm not quite sure what to do next. I feel confused. Help me come up with some ideas to move forward." Women say, "I'm so overwhelmed. I have so much to do. I don't even know where to begin. I'm stuck. Help!" See the difference? The man is looking for direction. The woman is voicing a cry of self-blame. Many women feel as if we should know how to do everything without ever asking for help. When faced with new choices and decisions, it's normal to feel confused. This is certainly true in business and marketing.

Owning a business is like one of the greatest self-growth seminars you will ever attend. You are challenged with decisions daily yet There's no road map. You need to stay sharp, observant and coming from a strong sense of self. Plus, we have too much to do. Speaker and author Brian Tracy says the average businessperson is 300-400 hours behind in reading, so you are not the only one with books you may never read.

We need time and attention for our families and loved ones, our business, our health, our home. On top of that, we are bombarded with endless marketing messages daily screaming: "Buy me! Choose me! You're not okay without me!" No wonder we feel stressed out and overwhelmed.

Overwhelm is fear that looks like having too many things to do. We don't know how to cope, so we go into "overload" or "overwhelm," and just stop. If overwhelm lasts longer than we want to tolerate, then we shift from saying, "I'm overwhelmed" to saying, "I'm stuck". The mistake many women make is believing our feelings of overwhelm are our fault.

Everyone needs escapism activities, and when I feel overwhelmed, my favorite "escapism" activity is shopping. I also love getting spa services such as a manicure or a facial. Or it could be playing with your children or walking with a friend.

Early one bright spring morning last year, our dear neighbor died instantly of a massive heart attack. He was like a family member and a gentle presence in our lives every day. And even though I had a looming deadline, I couldn't face working that week. I was saddened and emotionally overwhelmed. We'd had four deaths of people close to us that year but our neighbor was the dearest. I learned that when a person is grieving, there is less blood flow to the temporal region of the brain, making us feel overwhelmed and indecisive. That was me—the poster girl of overwhelm and indecision.

When you are grieving, find simple ways to reconnect with the beauty in nature or the smile of a child. If you enjoy exercise, this is not the time to stop. Physical activity will keep your endorphin levels up and help you feel alive in the midst of sadness. A mini-getaway can help you to find joy, passion and connection again. Breaks like a brisk walk or an afternoon at a favorite museum can help you feel refreshed and even solve the business challenges on your mind.

Yesterday, Maree, an intelligent, highly motivated woman, asked me, "Denise, I'm embarrassed to ask this but I'm feeling overwhelmed and out of it. What do you suggest?"

"Go with the flow. Let it be okay to not charge forward. Slow down long enough to receive." As women, our ability to reflect and recline helps us recharge our creative marketing batteries. Maree gave herself permission to take a break. She spent a relaxing day tending to her garden, an activity she loves. Working with her hands in the soil gave her a fresh perspective. She approached her business with renewed enthusiasm.

Are You Yin or Yang about "Overwhelm"?

I have worked with men who didn't know what to do and were okay with that. However, women often turn "not knowing" into a negative judgment about themselves and their abilities. I used to do it, too. Men consider "not knowing" part of being a business owner. It's not something to be afraid of; not having all the answers is just a part of life.

Many women feel they should do everything effortlessly, and visions of "Super Woman" still abound. Men readily accept their need for mentors even if they won't ask for driving directions. Women want to do everything without help.

The guidance of a mentor can be a wonderful thing. Think about who could possibly help you in your business. Usually mentors won't reach out and offer to help you, but if you ask, you may be happily surprised at their willingness to help someone like yourself who is on the way up. But you have to ask in a simple way. Don't ask for someone to make a big commitment of time. Instead ask for a small commitment, such as, "Gee, would it be okay for me to send you an email with a question now and then?" rather than, "Would you be willing to make me your protégé and teach me everything you know?" (To learn more about how to create a great mentoring relationship go to www.MarketingforHer.com, click on "Keyword Search and then click on "Great Mentoring Relationship.")

Multi-tasking? A Gift or a Curse?

There is another difference between the sexes that impacts our state of overwhelm. Scientists have found a physical difference that points to an important reason why women feel overwhelmed more than men.

Our brains have two hemispheres. The left hemisphere helps us handle cognitive information, numbers and data. The right hemisphere is our source of creativity, feelings, and intuition. There is a band of tissue connecting these two lobes of the brain called the *corpus callosum.* Studies have proven conclusively in women this tissue is slightly larger than in men, so women have more connections between the two hemispheres, whereas men's brains are more compartmentalized. A friend said, "Oh, so men's brains are like waffles and women's brains are like a dish of pasta."

This means women are better at multi-tasking. We handle combinations of things that make men dizzy just watching us. We've got a baby on one hip, while checking dinner in the oven and talking with a friend on the phone. No problem. We have a more integrated use of both left and right hemispheres. The upside is we are more balanced than men and we can do several things at once. Now you know why men, lovable as they are, seem like such plodding lummoxes. They rarely do more than one thing at a time. However they are often better at focusing on that one thing.

For the nurturing, house and home tasks most women still handle, multi-tasking is a gift. For a small business owner, multi-tasking helps you handle the details. However, focus and clarity are also necessities for business owners. You need focus to develop a marketing strategy, implement it and track your results. You need focus working with individual customers. You need focus to create cash flow and freedom. If you don't focus, what do you think happens? You guessed it – you feel overwhelmed.

Stop the Chattering Monkeys

Our brains race at about 1,500 words a minute, and we have on average 60,000 thoughts a day. Many of those words and thoughts are negative. A lot of people call this "monkey chatter." Monkey chatter is things like:

- "I didn't go to the gym and exercise today."
- "Don't forget to pick up the dry cleaning."
- "Why hasn't Sue hasn't called back? Maybe she's upset."
- "I need to meet with Billy's soccer coach. That guy is a jerk!"
- "It would be wonderful to get that new account. I'm not sure I can do it."
- "I forgot to pick up a gift for the party this weekend."
- "You dummy, you'll never figure this out. You're so behind."

Monkey chatter can weaken us. It prevents us from finishing projects. To get out of overwhelm and focus, first we must turn off the monkey chatter. But how? Set aside a time to create a plan. Take a few deep breaths and meditate or pray for a few minutes if it helps you clear your mind. Softly say, "The perfect solution is coming to me now."

As other things pop up in your mind, say, "It's okay. Right now, I am focusing on completing this." Then return to the task at hand. Stay in the present moment. When you're working on something outside your comfort zone, it's natural to want to do other things that provide instant gratification. Make a conscious choice to stay focused, even though your brain wants to wander.

As women, it is easy to over-nurture. It comes naturally. Why not make a batch of cookies for the kids before they come home? Why not call your spouse or partner and ask about his day? These are loving things we do effortlessly. But if we do them as a way of avoiding other tasks, they will keep us scattered and feeling overwhelmed. Besides, you and your kids don't need the cookies and you called your spouse earlier.

It's easier to pick up the dry cleaning, open the mail, re-arrange files, and call a friend, than to dig into a marketing plan or write a sales letter where you need to toot your horn. Your office is organized and your blouse is back from the dry cleaners for tomorrow's meeting, but you haven't figured out what to say. This can create anxiety and overwhelm especially when your tendency is to multitask rather than focus.

Practice selective procrastination. Ignore little things, just temporarily. Breathe and focus on one thing at a time. When you're in the present moment, you can use the full power of your mind to complete each activity. Fully-focused brainpower is a powerful thing. It doesn't require testosterone. You will make better decisions and accomplish more in less time when your energy is focused.

You actually accomplish more when you are focused. If you must, carry a tiny tape recorder to record your thoughts so you can play them back later. Or, make lists as ideas pop up. Successful people jump from one thing to the next without "down time." They clear their mind of excess thought and work purely on the task at hand. Be fully in the present moment. As you focus, you will discover you get more done than when you were multi-tasking and letting those 1,500 words a minute run amuck.

Limiting negative self-talk will make you feel luxurious, almost opulent. Your feelings of overwhelm will diminish. You will feel empowered. Feeling scattered and overwhelmed is a fear-based state of mind. You cannot do great things if you are in fear. Our minds solve problems best when we feel confident and enthusiastic.

Millionaires are wonderful when it comes to focusing on a project and getting it done. They kept their mind on one thing at a time. As I worked with millionaires, I envied their ability to focus. I thought, *Well, they have the luxury to do that. They're millionaires.* I did not envy their money. It was their freedom to think, vision, and create I wanted. Then I came to the conclusion I couldn't do any more in one day than I already was doing. We can only run so fast, right? So I decided to give it a try. I thought I would fall behind. Miraculously it didn't happen. Once I learned the power of living in the present moment, I solved problems faster. I got more done in a day than when I was constantly trying to juggle ten things at once. When you eliminate the monkey chatter and stop multi-tasking, you will feel this power, too. (To discover more tools to help you eliminate procrastination from your life, go to:

www.MarketingForHer.com, click on "Keyword Search" and then click on "Stop Procrastination Now.")

Think about it. You are on the phone with a client and you're thinking about:

- What's for dinner?
- Got to pick up the dry cleaning.
- I'm having a bad hair day.
- And myriad other annoying thoughts.

Can you give that important call your focus and attention under these conditions? No. Can your customer tell you're distracted? Yes. Will she want to do business with you if you seem scattered? No, of course not. Focus is a trait many successful business owners have in common. Use it to help you get more done and solve problems.

Here are twenty great questions from the book *The Magic in Asking the Right Questions* by Bill Mayer that can help you develop creative solutions. These questions can help you start thinking in ways that are more positive, less overwhelmed and more creative. They can help you solve problems and get better results. They are:

1. How can I make it fun?
2. What is great about this?
3. What am I thankful for?
4. What's a better way of looking at this?
5. What is my desired outcome?
6. What is a possible solution?
7. What did I learn from this?
8. How can I simplify this?
9. What would a power thinker do in this situation?
10. What's the best use of my time right now?
11. What action do I need to take?
12. Why do I want to do this?
13. What are the benefits?
14. How can I feel better right now?
15. How can I raise my energy level?
16. What do I want to accomplish today?
17. How can I be more productive?
18. What do I value most in my life?
19. What's a better choice to focus on?
20. What's a more empowering question to ask?

Thinking Outside the Box

Do you ever feel stuck in a box? Psychologist Dr. Warren Berland author of *Out of the Box for Life* says the chatter and self-doubt we experience are our ego at work. Our ego tries to protect us and help us deal with the world. However, it's almost always negative. Ego is not solution-oriented and is actually disempowering.

Traditional psychology focuses on what's wrong. It doesn't help people feel better. Berland realized therapy often took years and its effects were fleeting. He says, "The ego is a veil that obscures who we are. Our true nature resides just below the ego and is completely immune to whatever has scarred it."

Berland says we are our "True Self." Our true self asks questions and knows the answers. When we go beyond the ego, we allow our true self to expand and direct our actions. Berland explains, "From that vantage point, we see a different world, and experience ourselves in a radically new light." Our true selves can help us solve any issue. This is a creative place where great ideas live and you can do almost anything.

When I coach people who are unfocused, I ask them the following questions and listen to what they say and what they're passionate about.

- What are your special gifts you have to share with the world?
- What makes you unique?
- What do you offer that no one else has?
- What gifts do you possess that makes you special?

Your uniqueness is at the heart of your most compelling marketing message. When your purpose is irresistible, people want to play with you. They pick up on your enthusiasm and want to be aligned with you.

Testosterone-Free Tip: Get out of overwhelm by clearing the clutter in your mind. Expand your horizons and consider your choices – even those choices you believe to be 'unconventional.' One of our wonderful Yin qualities is that of reflecting and letting things come to us. Take time to reflect, with no expectations. It is amazing how exciting ideas and strategies can come to you when you slow down a little.

Summing It Up

§ If you feel stuck, stay active by looking for solutions to your marketing challenges.

§ Grief can increase feelings of overwhelm and indecisiveness. If you have suffered a loss, be patient with yourself and stay active.

§ Women are better at multi-tasking than men. For nurturing tasks, multi-tasking is a gift. In business, multi-tasking can leave you feeling unfocused and scattered.

§ Monkey chatter is usually negative. It is our subconscious mind or ego doing its job.

§ Take a deep breath and meditate, pray or make lists to help clear your mind.

§ Set aside time to complete a challenging task. Don't let anything interrupt you.

§ Work on your feared thing first.

Get Started Now

Listed below are strategies that will help you feel less overwhelmed.

§ Eliminate outside distractions in your work area.

§ Give your mind a place to play and create solutions to marketing challenges. Take time to vision and create.

§ Imagine you just woke from a coma. You don't remember friends, enemies, family, societal norms or expectations. You only remember what you're good at and what you love. What would you do? Forget everyone else's needs for a while and enjoy a positive marketing coma.

§ When you wrack your brain with how-to questions, the answers elude you. When you are open, often the answers drop into your lap, courtesy of your True Self.

Last Word:

Every great achievement is preceded by a vision so clear that you can almost taste it. What's your vision?

Chapter Seven

Thinking Bigger and Deserving Much More

"I like thinking big. If you're going to be thinking anything, you might as well think big."

— Donald Trump

Having a big dream is a wonderful thing to inspire you and spur you forward. In this chapter you will learn the secrets to develop a Clear Compelling Vision.

Additionally, you will shift your thinking from owning a business to creating freedom. I doubt you chose to go into business to work longer hours and get less pay, did you? As you read, you will see how to create a business that runs without your constant presence. You will learn to focus on the things that matter and delegate other tasks.

Playing Small Doesn't Serve the World – or You

As women, we tend to place our most importance on the quality of our relationships. Relationships are high on our list of must-haves. We put pride and energy into creating relationships that form a support network. Statistics show when women go through a life trauma, such as a death, divorce or job loss, we handle the change better because we have a circle of friends and family. We draw on their strength. Ever notice how men mostly have wives or girlfriends and almost no other support system?

Unfortunately while we're busy building wonderful support networks, we often neglect our business or career. We know Prince Charming is dead. But our dreams of abundance don't always get off the ground because we're nourishing friendships instead of our pocketbooks. It's easier to rush to a friend than to make a sales call. As a result, many of us play a smaller game of life. Playing small no longer serves you or the world. When you play a larger game of life, you get to enjoy the life you imagined when you started your business.

It's time to create a Clear Compelling Vision for your life and your business. Imagine it is two years from now. In Chapter Fourteen you will write a shorter-range goal, but right now let's go for the big one. The whole enchilada.

Imagine living in your dream home. Would you live in an oceanfront home on the beach? Or an elegant 5,000-square-foot, "cabin" in the mountains? Or, would you choose a New York penthouse?

Write out what it would be like living in the home of your dreams two years from now. Imagine yourself feeling happy, safe and loved. Write about what that home would be like and how you would feel living there. As you write, look back on how it all started from today. Start writing right now. Give yourself permission to dream.

However, your Clear Compelling Vision is about more than your dream home. Write about your life in this home in full sensory detail. What do you see, hear, smell, taste, and touch? In full detail, write about your gratitude at coming so far in just two years. . Write how great it feels to help the people who matter most. Don't let doubt get in your way as you write. As you write do not look up. Don't correct yourself, just keep writing.

Now visualize living your dream life. This is the most important part of your Clear Compelling Vision. Think about what it would be like to enjoy your perfect day. Who do you work with? What kind of environment do you work in? What do you do all day? What do you wear? Do you travel? Do you work at home?

Write in detail what it's like to be you. Do you have a housekeeper? An assistant? A personal trainer? What is it like to deal with people who are warm and gracious, and appreciate you as you are? Imagine two years from now looking back on today. Think about how grateful you are for taking the right steps so you can enjoy the life you have today. Let your vision and thoughts flow until you are finished with your Clear Compelling Vision. How do success and prosperity feel? Most people stay in their comfort zone because they cannot "see" what it would be like to live a more abundant lifestyle. Your Clear Compelling Vision helps you do just that. So stop reading, and right now, grab paper and pen, and start writing. Let it take as long as it takes.

Would you like to read a Clear Compelling Vision that I wrote several years ago? Not only will it inspire you, but it will also give you an example. The exciting part is that most of that vision has come true for me. (To read it, go to www.MarketingForHer.com, click on "Keyword Search" and then "Clear Compelling Vision.")

Do You Want to Buy a Job or Create Freedom?

If you have already started your business, consider what you do with your time. Are you slaving to keep customers happy? Or are you in command of your life and your time?

In my *Testosterone Free Marketing* workshops and teleseminars, I meet amazing women. However, many succeed in simply creating not a business, but a job. Worse, many create a job that offers no security and pays less than the jobs they left. They tell me while they are working for a client they are so busy that they don't have time to market. When that client's work is wrapped up, they must start marketing again to find another. They do everything possible to avoid marketing until they have no choice. Does this sound like you?

One woman, an artist, created hand-painted silks. Several boutiques carried her wares. She wondered how she could experience financial success while painting silks. I asked if she could mount her silks in frames and sell them to galleries for much higher prices than clothing. She said she wanted her silk to be wearable art, something to be used. I asked if she was willing to teach others to paint silk while she got her product in more stores. She insisted her joy came from the painting the fabric. This woman was in love with her product. Her business was an expensive hobby and would not let her to grow past the number of silks she could personally paint and sell.

Often shifting the vision of the business you originally wanted to something more visionary and less hands-on can make a positive difference in the amount of money you create. When you are caught up in doing, doing, doing, you are acting more like an employee and less like a Chief Executive Officer. Many home-based entrepreneurs are in love with their product, service or process, and not in love with the idea of running a business. Many of us love what we do. It brings us a feeling of accomplishment, but we haven't shifted to being a CEO. The work you do may be the work you weren't paid enough for as an employee.

Now you own a business and you are working harder than ever. You do everything possible to make customers happy. You don't commute to work anymore or punch a time clock. But you still don't have financial freedom. Instead you've bought a job. You're working "in" your business and not "on" your business as Michael Gerber author of *The E-Myth: Why Most Businesses Fail and What to Do About It* says.

Gerber explains business owners must shift from being a Technician or Manager to becoming a true Entrepreneur. Technicians and Managers "do tasks." Entrepreneurs vision and try new ideas. Though you probably will wear all the hats and do everything at the beginning, start with the end in mind. The goal of a business is to create a self-sustaining system that works with or without you. A business like this is an asset that can be sold to another owner in the future. This is one way to create wealth.

Owning a business is about moving energy to create something new. Move energy one direction and create one result. Move energy another direction and create a different result.

What you would like your business to provide you? What did you envision when you started? Maybe you didn't see a massive enterprise. Maybe you enjoy making beautiful gift baskets or helping people balance their checking accounts. Maybe you thought your job was finding more customers so you can gradually raise your rates.

Is doing, doing, doing bringing you financial freedom? Could you leave your business for a while without revenues dropping off? Or, are you in bondage to your business? In our race to multi-task and be all things to all people, many women discover they have spread themselves too thin. Perhaps you never imagined marketing and getting new customers would take so much time. And you can't run any faster with all your responsibilities to your businesses and your family.

The business model you create can contribute to your success. Look to build a business that provides residual income. Rents are one example, royalties or subscription fees are another. Also businesses where jobs are systemized can create income that keeps rolling in, whether you're at the office or not. A business like this helps you focus your time and energy on the highest and best use of your time. Now is the time to slow down and take a serious look at what you want to create.

Work Smarter, Not Harder

Ask yourself what you want your clients to get from the experience of doing business with you. This is different from thinking about what you want from your business. It is a change in focus to thinking how you affect the lives of your customers. Rather than be in love with producing silk scarves or spreadsheets, you find extra ways to enhance the lives of your customers. Don't fall in love with your product or your service. Instead, fall in love with your customer. There is more discussion of this concept in Chapter Eleven.

The Highest and Best Use of Your Time

I have a part-time assistant who files, types, and runs myriad errands. I have a virtual assistant who does technical things I do not want to learn how to do. I have a housekeeper who comes in two mornings a week. My housekeeper is wonderful at organizing and cleaning. As a business owner, my time is worth more than a housekeeper and your time is more valuable, too.

House cleaning is the first task every woman should delegate to others. Stop thinking of it as a luxury and start thinking of yourself as a CEO. If you do your own housekeeping, you value your time at the rate of a housekeeper. Also, at an appropriate age, your children should be responsible for picking up after themselves and doing other chores that contribute to the family.

When you accept the help of others, you will feel more on-purpose. Marketing your business and getting the word out will be easier because you have delegated unimportant tasks that crowded your time. Marketing will always be one of the most important parts of your business. Whether it's thinking about what marketing strategies you want to put into place or going on sales calls, these are the activities that should come first, ahead of dusting, answering emails and doing household tasks.

If you have just started your business, hiring part-time help may sound unrealistic. But keep the end goal in mind. Do the work that is the highest and best use of your time. If you only hire a housekeeper one afternoon a month, that's four more hours to spend on your business. Or, spend half that time on your business and half doing something fun with your family. The ease you will feel when you walk past your sparkling bathrooms and freshly dusted and vacuumed living room will help you feel prosperous and successful.

Enroll Others in Your Dream

Many people don't have a big dream or a vision like you do. Perhaps they did once long ago, but they have long since put it aside. When people don't have a dream, it's not difficult to get them excited about your dream. You might be amazed to discover how many people will follow your lead because they do not have their own vision. If you imbue your vision with energy, passion, and enthusiasm, it's easy to enroll support. Your enthusiasm and passion will get customers and others interested in your products and services as well as your business. When you have enough cash flow coming in and you have organized your business so others support you, your business can run itself. .

Imagine the freedom you would feel if you sold your business because you had created a system. How great would it be to have six or seven figures stashed away because you sold your business and now you can do what you want? Do you want to leverage that money into another business? Do you want to travel? Do you want to start a charity? Now you have choices.

Passion is important but the only reason to start a business is to make money. You will not get there constantly staring at your computer, nose to the grindstone finishing a customer's job, without planning how to grow your business so you can eventually step away as money rolls in.

Who are the wealthiest self-made people? Most people agree Hollywood celebrities make the greatest amount of money fastest. But how? It's not just the millions of dollars from one movie that makes them rich. It's the residual income they make on the success of that movie that makes them wealthy. It's not the concert tour that makes the singer wealthy but the residual income on every T-shirt and DVD sold. How do they command that attention in the first place? It's marketing. They do it themselves or they are surrounded by a team of experts.

How do you create a business that will help you build freedom and income, if not fame? With businesses that provide residual income. These can include:

- Rents from real estate. Whether you rent a spare bedroom or become a real estate tycoon, rentals provide income you work with and then the positive cash keeps rolling in.

- Royalties from the sale of books and other inte erty. You don't have to write and publish a boo alty income. Ebooks, tapes, CDs and other i products that share your expertise or others can ...nge the lives of others and be highly profitable.

- Products people purchase over and over. Think lotions and potions. Vitamins and beauty products. This is how the network marketing industry has grown. What products do people use over and over that you can provide?

- A product where someone purchases a subscription and buys over and over again. Did you know there are now subscription websites that provide information about something you want to know about for a monthly fee. One example is www.MarketingforHer.com.

- Leverage your money and get it working for you. Get savvy about investing.

- How about franchises or licensing? If you have made your business successful, you can turn it into a turnkey system so others can succeed in the same business. You get a percentage of income and you don't lift a finger to work in those businesses. It's a hands-off way to grow a business.

- Sell an awesome idea and make a royalty on each unit sold. If you patent a product, you might find a company looking for new products to manufacture and market. Some companies will buy a product for a flat fee. Other times they pay a fee and a royalty on each unit sold.

- If your business doesn't generate residual income, make your income more residual by creating duplicatible systems as defined by Gerber.

(If you would like to learn more about creating a business model that will help you to create financial freedom and wealth, go to www.MarketingForHer.com, click on "Keyword Search" and then click on "Business Model for Success.")

Summing It Up

- Playing small no longer serves you.
- Have you created a job or a business? How can you shift from being an "employee" in your business and move into the role of CEO?
- Your goal is not to be indispensable. Your goal is to create a business that works whether you do or not.
- Focus on the highest and best use of your time.
- Marketing will always be one of your highest and best uses of your time as a CEO. Even if you feel overwhelmed marketing, it is still a high return activity for you. When you have created marketing and sales systems that work effectively, then you can consider hiring other people to do it for you.
- Helpers can ease your stress and provide more quality time for you, your business and your family.
- Since most people don't have a dream, create an exciting vision to enroll other people in your dream.

Get Started Now

* If you have not yet done the Clear Compelling Vision exercise start now. Write from the perspective that you are living your ideal life in your dream house.
* Read your Clear Compelling Vision daily. This is a critical step toward making your business and your ideal day your reality.
* List the tasks you do. Organize them according to what price per hour they would command if you hired them out. Decide which could be hired out for the lowest hourly expense. Housekeeping is the first job to check off your list.
* Start simple. Could you get a high school or college student to file and ship orders? Would an older child be excited to help mom and make extra money?
* Think of ways to shift household to afford at least one helper. Are there little extras you spend money on that if you stopped would give you the money you need?
* Make a list of questions relevant to the kind of work the person will be doing and interview several candidates. Hire the one person you think is best suited.
* Make sure some of the time you save goes into marketing.

Last Word:

Someone asked a wise man which direction to take in life. The wise man asked, "What's your vision for the future?" The person said, "I don't have one."

The wise man replied, "Well, it doesn't matter which direction you take. Just about any road you take will get you there."

Chapter Eight

Marketing Is Yang and Women Are Yin

"Yang cannot exist by itself; it can exist only when it is supported by yin. Hence yin is the foundation of yang. Similarly, yin cannot alone manifest itself; it can manifest itself only when accompanied by yang. Hence yang is the expression of yin".

— Chang Tsai

If you feel most marketing is too pushy, join the club. With women, I often see avoidance and acute discomfort around marketing because they do not want to be annoying or manipulative. I meet women with excellent people skills who enjoy networking and building relationships. However, they stop short of creating a "yes" for themselves, their business, and their customers. Using the Yang energy required to project outward feels strange and unfamiliar, but once you "get it," you will enjoy incredible success.

News Flash! Marketing Is Mostly "A Guy Thing"

Women who are naturally great at marketing and selling often grow up with a strong role model who taught her to value what she said. She may have had a parent or family member in business who was influential in her life. Or, she may have had brothers and had to speak up for herself. These women love to talk and they have no problem asking for the business. Even if you were told you had value, if your mother was quiet and lacked confidence, you may have modeled that behavior rather than what you were told.

When men have challenges with marketing and selling, it's often because they lack relationship-building skills. Women excel at relationship-building. But we are often so busy nurturing friendships that we won't ask a customer a buying question to steer them towards a "yes."

The "Guy Way" Is Not Our Way

Marketing is not rocket science. But, as one woman said at a "testosterone heavy" marketing seminar, "Learning about it and doing it are two different things."

"Putting yourself out there" is not difficult to understand. But it is outside of how we think of ourselves. There is a flow to how things occur in business. Marketing moves products and services from you to your customer. Your role is to encourage that flow in a positive way. A win for the customer. And a win for you. That is a win-win. If money is not flowing in, you are blocking the flow.

The masculine way of getting a business started is often different from our way. Let's say John and Jane are in comparable circumstances, and both are ready to start a business. Both have a computer and $5,000 to start.

Typically, John drags a folding table in from the garage and borrows a chair from the kitchen. He picks up a battered filing cabinet from a garage sale. It doesn't have to look perfect; customers will not be coming to his office. He will go to them. He sets up an arrangement with a responsible teen to help him package and ship products from his garage two afternoons a week after school. He buys cardstock and prints inexpensive business cards on his computer. Most of his dollars are invested in small, repetitive advertisements. He learns to write a powerful sales letter and gets it on an inexpensive Internet site. He forms an alliance with several people who have focused opt-in lists of email addresses. He agrees to pay them a commission on sales if they run a short article in their email newsletter with a link to his sales letter. Orders start coming in and his business is off to a small, but promising start.

Compare this to how I've seen many women start businesses:

First Jane shops for the perfect desk and chair. She wants to have a pleasant place to work and impress a client who might drop by. She buys a brand new file cabinet and spends hours setting up the perfect filing system. She finds a graphic designer who designs the perfect logo and business card. She ponders the right shade of peach for weeks. (One friend of mine literally went through three designers and spent four months on this task.) She creates an elegant brochure or attractive website. She calls friends and tells them she has started a business. She attends networking meetings and politely mingles. She goes home and waits for orders. When an order comes in, she ships it out. It's a slow, frustrating journey.

Whose business will start producing revenue faster? John's or Jane's?

I've seen books for women on how to start a home-based business that include an entire chapter on how to pick out ergonomically correct furniture. Another chapter was devoted to setting up the perfect filing system. Is this business by *Better Homes & Gardens*? Another book advised lining up the right certified public accountant, a banker, a tax attorney and organizing your office. Only one chapter was about Marketing. There is merit to having a team of advisors, but without a strong marketing focus, those advisors will never be needed.

Testosterone-Free Tip: Perfection is impossible but, as women, we often feel like failures if we do not try to be perfect. Getting everything "perfect" before taking action is a way of avoiding rejection. Be satisfied with 80 percent and then move on. You will be amazed at what you can accomplish when you skip the futile pursuit of perfection.

Marketing and Masculinity are about Projecting Outward

I was talking with my friend Jim and I shared with him my feeling that marketing is very masculine. Jim replied, "Let's face it, Denise, marketing is more than just masculine; it is downright penile."

I shared Jim's comment with another male friend. He replied, "Marketing is very yang, very masculine. In fact, marketing is the *most* masculine business activity."

Masculinity is about outwardly projecting. It goes right down to physiology. Marketing is also about outwardly projecting. Consider activities commonly considered masculine, or yang. War is yang. Hunting is yang. Sports are yang. Throw that ball. Block that tackle. It's all outwardly projecting. Scientific studies are learning that although conditioning plays an important role in who we are as men and women, gender goes far beyond the obvious physical differences to how we think, communicate and solve problems. We know this in our personal relationships and in the corporate office. But

Testosterone-Free Marketing is the first book that acknowledges this fact of life when it comes to marketing our home-based businesses.

Men don't enjoy rejection but they accept it as part of adult life. If they don't project outward and ask for what they want, they will not have a satisfying life. A boy tries out for a sports team and is accepted or declined. A teen boy asks a teen girl for a date and she accepts or declines. A man asks a woman to marry. A man makes sexual overtures. A man asks for a raise. Men are taught they must ask or suffer a lousy life. If they are turned down, they will often try again later. They will try another strategy. Achieving for men is about asking for what they want.

Women are raised avoid rejection at all costs. We are taught to look great, wait patiently and be "a good girl." We hope to get noticed and be given what we want. Our appearance is more deeply linked to who we are and how others perceive us. If we do not get what we want, it is impolite to ask. We internalize and feel rejection more deeply. Achieving for women traditionally was about being nice and being pretty.

Femininity Is about Waiting to Receive

Women are about opening, nurturing and receiving. We bake cookies or light candles to make home more inviting. Women wait to receive. Here are examples of masculine "projecting outward" and feminine "waiting to receive:

- Men are about *Sports Illustrated*; women are about *Redbook.*
- Men are about *Fortune* magazine; women are about *Vogue.*
- Men are about spy novels; women are about romance novels.
- Men are about David Letterman; women are about Oprah Winfrey.

- Men are about Fantasy Sports Camp; women are about a tropical beach and being served drinks by a handsome waiter.
- Men are about action movies; women are about romance movies.
- Men are about Home Depot; women are about Nordstrom.
- Men want tools for Christmas; women want Chanel No. 5.
- Men want to watch the game; women want an afternoon at the spa
- Men are about asking and nudging; women are about holding back, demurring, and finally saying "yes."

Even after years of feminism, most of us still bristle at overtly aggressive women. In our media, seriously aggressive business women always lose. Women have a narrow tightrope to walk and pay a heavy price for behavior outside that acceptable range. They are disliked by everyone. Assertive men are hailed as go-getters; assertive women are nicknamed "Barracuda" behind their backs.

A friend of mine describes marketing as a dart and dartboard. Tom can't understand why some people choose to be the dartboard in search of flying darts. "Marketers should be darts," Tom says. Meaning he cannot fathom why someone would not take an aggressive stance when marketing their business. His view does not take into consideration how harshly women are judged for the same behavior that is considered normal and acceptable for men.

Claudia said, "I would rather my marketing draw in customers like a powerful magnet." That's what "the power of attraction" is all about. *Testosterone Free Marketing* is about getting your yin and yang in balance so your marketing works like a powerful magnet … which is more comfortable for most women than trying to be a dart. When you let your yang side come out and play, you can enjoy asking for what you want with a sense of fearlessness and entitlement.

In August of 1997, I walked up to the man who became my soulmate, and started a conversation at a beach picnic. After a few minutes of conversation while standing in a throng of people, I asked him directly, "Who wants to go for a swim?" I wanted to talk with him away from the others. He said, "Sounds great. I'll go for a swim." It worked. However, if he had not asked for my phone number and called me later, I never would have seen him again. He had to project outward and take things to the next step. We are still happily together.

The feminist movement told women that we should not have to wait to receive. That to do so was putting ourselves in a subservient role. We should take control and ask a man for a date. . . . Except this deprives men of their need to outwardly project and pursue. The best-selling book *The Rules* by Fein & Schneider in 1996 basically affirms that men's natural role is to be the hunter-gatherer and outwardly project. The woman's role is to wait back in the cave, ready to receive.

I'm alarmed by the sexual forwardness of young women today in the new millennium. They are much more readily "available" to young men and communicate that in no uncertain terms. There is no romance or wooing. The men don't have to pursue. This is merely my opinion – and I'm not a sociologist – but I think there may be a link between the behavior of sexually overt young women and the lyrics of rap and hip-hop music that refer to women by terms that were formerly not used in polite company. Men do not value what they don't have to work for.

According to the rules, you never call a man you are interested in. And never talk more than ten minutes on the phone. Even in romantic movies today, the leading man doesn't truly value the woman until he must pursue her.

Many women feel these rules are cruel, calculated and harsh. What feels right to a man sends a woman into orbit. Until very recently, women didn't generally pursue. And I believe that is still the exception and not the norm. We do the attracting. Men, are brought up to get out there and ask for what they want. When it comes to our personal relationships, attracting and waiting to receive is often still be the best strategy for women. The drawback is: Waiting to receive generally does not work in business. Pursuing in business is extremely uncomfortable for many women. Business has no gender; however the people in it do.

Recently I re-watched the movie, *First Wives Club*. Three women with successful husbands are taken advantage of in divorce and vow revenge. Their big success comes when they redecorate a dumpy building into a center to help other divorcees. They throw an elegant party, forcing the ex-husbands to pay the tab. What is totally yin is how they measure success: a charity effort, a fancy decorating job and a big party.

One woman pulls off a takeover of her husband's advertising agency by buying his partner's share. However this doesn't produce as many whoops and hollers as the newly-decorated office and party. What's going on? Women bring to their home-based businesses the same nurturing and nesting characteristics they use at home. They also bring their skills and expertise. But, outwardly projecting is out of our comfort zone.

"It never hurts to ask!" is a saying you will most likely hear from a man. The masculine role of projecting outward and making the first move is easier and more natural to men.

"I shouldn't have to aaaaask!" women exclaim in frustration. Expecting others to read your mind is risky in relationships and disastrous in business. In business, we *must* ask. Otherwise we wait for customers like we waited by the phone for the cute boy in history class to call us for a date.

In her book *EVEolution: The Eight Truths of Marketing to Women* author Faith Popcorn says in truth number three: "If She Has to Ask, It's Too Late." Popcorn says, "Maybe our reticence to express our needs is part of a learned behavior, honed in the classroom. According to a recent study by the American Association of University Women, girls start getting quieter in sixth grade and drop to minimum levels of participation by the seventh and eighth grades. Or maybe we pick up signals earlier, learning that saying, 'I want' or, 'I need' seems unladylike and unattractive."

Testosterone-Free Tip: If you don't ask, you won't get what you want. Take a deep breath and remind yourself that you are entitled to ask. If you're going to be yang enough to start a business you need to be yang enough to project outwardly.

Girls and boys are conditioned to behave differently. Boys outwardly project. Girls are often told not to toot their own horn or to wait to be noticed. There may have been serious consequences if you did not follow the rules. You may have been judged for speaking out. Or, love and acceptance was withheld if you weren't "a nice girl."

Every time you heard, "Don't toot your own horn" or, "Let the boy win" or, "Let others go first," you were taught behaviors the opposite of what you need to do to successfully get the word out about your business. That's why, when you read books on marketing in the past, you felt uncomfortable but did not know why. This feminine conditioning may be holding you back from the success you deserve in your business.

Popcorn's fifth truth is: "Walk, Run, Go to Her, Secure Her Loyalty Forever." We like to be wooed. We want others to outwardly project while we receive. As business owners, it's our turn to go to our customers and secure their loyalty. It's our job to outwardly project.

Women's magazines often include articles on, "How to Get What You Want from Your Man." These articles are usually about learning to ask. Why do magazines keep running these articles? Because asking for what we want and need still makes many of us squirm. Every day, millions of women sigh heavily and protest, "I shouldn't have to aaaaask!"

(To discover more about the amazing differences between women and men in business, go to www.MarketingForHer.com, click on "Keyword Search" and then click on "Vive La Difference.")

New Conscious Choices, Not Old Knee-Jerk Reactions

How do you do that? Stop letting knee-jerk reactions hold you back. Then make different conscious choices. When you need to call someone and your hands are getting clammy and you would rather check your emails, you can make a different conscious choice. When you know it would make sense to send out a sales letter but you cannot bring yourself to write the letter because you will sound "too big for your britches," you can make a different choice. Is your hesitation because it's not the right thing to do, or is it because someone told you that "nice girls don't toot their own horn?"

If you understand and truly implement the concept of making different conscious choices, you will be well on the way to success in your business and in your life. Getting out of your fears is all about making different conscious choices. Yet women still ask me, "Okay, but how do I do that?"

Here's the answer: stop, consider your reaction and ask, "Is this choice serving me? Is it leading to success or is it keeping me stuck?" Your intuition will tell you the answers. You may still be afraid. But you will know the best course of action. You may need to "practice the future" and "act as if" you are a confident woman. What you need to do is probably not technically difficult but simply saying the words is outside your comfort zone.

Even though we need to get the word out, we do not have to do it in "testosterone heavy" ways. You will learn in Chapter Twelve you can avoid the "guns and grenades" marketing methods, and learn marketing strategies that help you be a powerful magnet.

Be a Woman of Action Rather than a "Lady in Waiting"

Marjorie Shaevitz author of *The Confident Woman* adds, "Because of years of female socialization, some women don't think they have the right to do what they want." She calls them "ladies in waiting." They are waiting for something to happen before they are willing to assert themselves and confidently. Shaevitz says, "Unlike women, men are not brought up to deny their desires … therefore there is a profound disconnection for men when they hear women aren't doing what they want."

Marketing is about asking for what you want. Entrepreneurial success is not measured by how well we apply our nurturing skills; it is measured by sales and profits. Business will come to us when we let people know we are here, we are competent and we are ready.

(To learn another secret about making new conscious choices that work better for you and your business, go to:

www.MarketingForHer.com, click on "Keyword Search" and then click on "Emotional Freedom.")

Testosterone Free Tip: Ask questions so customers tell you why it would be in their best interest to buy. Self-discovery is powerful. When customers tell you why they should buy, they sell to themselves. This is more powerful and easy. I often ask questions like: What do you want to create? What are your important goals? Does this make sense to you? This is a more yin approach that is amazingly helpful for customers.

Yin/Yang Quadrants

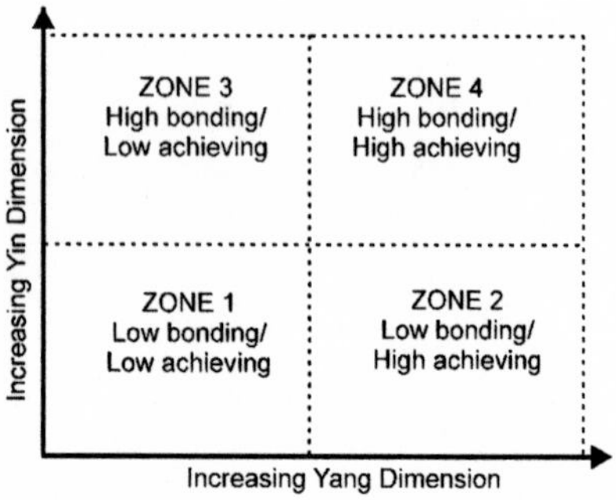

If we represent yin/yang visually, we could show the yang dimension going horizontally and the yin dimension going vertically:

- *Yang* dimension is driven by the numbers—more sales, more new accounts, most sales per month, etc., with focus on the "quantity" of business, but with less emphasis on the "quality" of business.
- *Yin* dimension is driven by the degree of bonding with clients—their sense of having their needs understood and taken care of, with focus on the "quality" of business, with increasing *depth* leading to repeat business but with less emphasis on the "quantity" of new business.

This representation gives us four quadrants, or zones:

1. Zone 1, with low bonding and low achieving. Finding someone in this zone in the field of marketing would be unlikely.
2. Zone 2, with low bonding but high achieving is the high testosterone zone, the rabid go-getter of new accounts competing against others of the same ilk—the very thing we're trying to avoid.

3. Zone 3, with high bonding but low achieving is the focal point of this book—how to raise the achievement drive without the testosterone side-effects.

4. Zone 4, with high bonding and high achieving is the ideal, but again without the testosterone. Becoming a goal-oriented achiever without sacrificing your drive for bonding is the whole point of this book.

Summing It Up

§ Marketing has mostly been about projecting outward and "A Guy Thing."

§ Marketing is counter to how we were conditioned growing up as girls.

§ Many women are waiting for customers to call like we waited for the cute boy in high school history class to call us for a date.

§ There is a flow in business. Products and services flow from a business to a customer. You are not "bad" or selfish for wanting to be paid fairly.

§ Marketing is a masculine or yang activity and is all about projecting outward

§ Femininity is about waiting to receiving, reflecting and creating.

§ Women often bring to their businesses the same nesting, nurturing, and waiting to receive characteristics they have used in their personal lives.

Get Started Now

Here are a few simple steps:

* Even if as a girl you were trained to not ask. You can and should direct people to buy your product or service and get paid fairly.
* When you sense uneasiness about picking up the phone or asking for an order, you are being "a girl." Make more assertive and less tentative choices. You can project outward and be pleasant and friendly, not confrontational or rude.
* Think how to ask for what you want so both people win. Help people come to their own conclusions about why they should buy.
* Rehearse by reading into a tape recorder or with a trusted friend. Get feedback.
* What can you shift to sound better to your customer? Could you use more energy in your voice? A smile? Will your customer understand what you are suggesting?
* Be warm, gracious, and a powerful, attracting magnet. Confidently say, "Usually at this point what our customers like to do is sign the agreement and provide a deposit check." Lead them to what you want them to do.
* Whatever response you hear, do not take it personally. As you get more comfortable, "No" will turn more frequently into "Yes."

Last Word:

If a prospective client or customer could benefit from your product or service, you are doing them a favor by telling them about it, so don't hold back and deny them the opportunity to buy from you.

Chapter Nine

Unleashing Your Feminine Force as a Marketer

"Remember, Ginger Rogers did everything Fred Astaire did, but she did it backwards and in high heels."

— Faith Whittlesey

Using your feminine force is not about unbuttoning an extra button on your blouse. It's not about slow Marilyn Monroe winks, high heels and a short skirt.

Traditionally, marketing was about masculine yang energy and projecting outward. But, being too "yang" gives marketers a bad reputation. For instance, what do you think about telemarketers? How about car salesmen? Pushy, obnoxious, rude? These are examples of too much yang energy and not enough yin energy. Successful marketing requires a comfortable balance between yin and yang energy.

Our Secret Advantage - Understanding Your Power

I am not a provocative dresser. Stilettos have been banished from my closet. I have short, dark hair and brown eyes. Even a Wonderbra wouldn't give me cleavage. Do you get my drift? I'm forever on a diet and I am not flirtatious. For years I have jokingly said I give off "housewife energy."

My friend Debbie is a successful realtor and a natural man-magnet. Recently, she asked my opinion on three photographs she was considering for her business card. Two were appropriate; in the third, she was wearing a come-hither look, bedroom hair, and cleavage. She thought the more provocative picture was an attention grabber. I asked, "What are you selling?" Women initiated contact with her more than men for business. She wisely chose a more conservative picture.

In the 1980s, women tried valiantly to be taken seriously. We wore linebacker shoulder pads and thought we could be more powerful by acting like men. Who could blame us? We didn't have any powerful female role models. Thankfully, we now recognize our differences are not shortfalls, but merely differences.

Testosterone-Free Tip: Being inauthentic is not the road to success and making more money in your business. Be yourself. There are benefits and gifts that being a woman can bring … if you know how to use them. This chapter will show you how.

In Gail Evens book *Play Like a Man -Win Like a Woman*, she asserts that in the corporate world, we play the mother, daughter, wife or mistress role. There are advantages and disadvantages to each.

§ **Daughter**: "If an older man turns you into a Daughter, you can profit in innumerable ways. You'll be exposed to people and places that others won't see, and you'll be privy to conversations that will give you insight into how the business is run. The downside? Men never think of their daughters as equals."

§ **Wife:** "Here you can be accepted on the job (more or less). But you're also encumbered with all the baggage a guy brings to the office from his real-life marriage. If he's married to a nagging woman, and you inadvertently start using language that reminds him of her, he'll probably respond by shutting you down."

§ **Mother:** "She's the secretary who's been at the company 37 years, the woman who's been the city editor for three decades, or the executive who's had the same title since 1975. Mothers get things done by innuendo and manipulation. The good part is: No boss can fire his mother."

§ **Mistress:** "As younger, more ambitious women have entered the workforce, the newer role is that of Mistress. You get to be a risk taker, make decisions and join the power structure, but you have to be very careful, because you're walking the tightrope of sexual tension."

When you step out of the corporate office and into your own business, the dog-eat-dog competition for the corner office no longer exists. People in their own enterprises do business with people they like and respect. Roles shift and people are generally not as competitive and wary of each other.

New Roles for a New World

I do my best when I create a different role with men. The *fifth* role is that of **Sister**. I am supportive and gracious and I'm straight forward. A sister can be light-hearted one moment and lay it on the line the next. Most men respect their sisters. They want what's best for them. They can talk without sexual tension.

Men are always projecting outward when they are around each other. Watch two men together. Until they know and trust each other, they circle each other like caged lions. Both are on guard. Perhaps this is why men don't form the same close friendships as women. On the other hand, men respect and admire women who are strong, capable and still feminine. Not tough. If you are a woman who gets things done no matter what the obstacles, you will be perceived as strong. If you are graciously persistent and capable of turning "No" into "Yes" so both people win, you will be seen as strong. If you have a positive attitude and smile, even in the face of adversity, you will be viewed as strong. Men love doing business with strong women – not tough ones!

Women are generally thought of as more trustworthy and more empathetic. In the world of entrepreneurs, men generally don't feel on the defensive around women. As a woman, you have advantages men don't have. Ernie and I used to do part-time real estate investing. Every week we would send a letter to homeowners regarding our services. The letter included both our names. When people called, they usually asked for me and not Ernie. Why? Women are often more comfortable dealing with other women, and men are often more comfortable dealing with women. They are not threatened by you, they can count on you to get results and they trust you. Use this to your advantage.

Testosterone-Free Tip: Do not hesitate to touch a man in a non-sexual way. When you want to make your point stick, touch his upper arm. Let your touch linger for a few seconds as you speak. Most men will be riveted to you. It is viewed as a gesture of support when accompanied with a smile. Use your femininity to your advantage.

Walking the Tightrope

Women walk a fine tightrope between being seen as feminine and being respected by men in business. If you want him to trust you as an advisor, don't be flirtatious or sexual. Be attractive, but in a business-like, professional way. Let your personality and enthusiasm convey your femininity rather than a plunging neckline and jangling jewelry.

Some women think men will be threatened if you tell him something constructive or point out an area where there is room for improvement. It's all in your delivery. Use a kind voice and smile. How do you say these things to your husband or mate? You wait until the time is right. You give him sincere praise first. You make your point. Then you give him a little more praise. Some men won't fess up to their shortcomings right away, but later they'll come to you and act like it was all their own idea.

There is a formula for giving constructive feedback. It goes like this:

- Compliment
- Compliment
- Constructive Comment
- Overall Compliment

You must communicate information so it is well received. The receiver will see you as credible when you compliment him first.

Discovering Your Customer's Core Values

As women we do an excellent job using our intuitive skills to "read" people. Pay attention to your customer's style of relating and doing business. That's how he or she will enjoy doing business with you. You may be doing business with a bottom-line "just the facts, ma'am" kind of person. If your tendency is to chit-chat and have a heart connection first, your style will make a fast-paced person impatient. If your pace is rapid-fire and you're dealing with a person whose style is leisurely, slow down.

A homework assignment that marital counselors often give couples is to make a list of caring behaviors that make each person feel loved and appreciated. Then do at least one caring behavior from your mate's list daily. If you pay attention to how your customer or client deals with you and others, you can show them appropriate caring behaviors in a business environment by dealing with them the way they want to be dealt with.

Did you know you can get a customer to happily say "yes" before even telling them what you offer? One of the most powerful facts you can know about a person is their core values. Core values are stronger than goals. People often set goals that are not congruent with who they are. Sometimes our goals are set to please someone else – a spouse, a parent or a boss, for example. Goals are something we would like to have. Core values are the essence of who we are. We must have them to be reasonably satisfied. For example, if someone's core values include integrity, he can be trusted to not lie to gain advantage. (This does not mean he will reveal the whole truth, but what he does reveal will be honest and true to the best of his or her understanding.)

When you elicit core values, you are having a conversation that usually goes unsaid in our business day. This conversation is at the heart of what motivates us to buy and say "yes." It's why we get out of bed in the morning. It's why we do what we do. It's what we want to accomplish before we die. Ask these simple Core Values Questions and you will have a powerful advantage to help you get to "yes" faster. Because women are usually seen as trustworthy, we can usually ask personal questions without seeming intrusive.

Let's say you meet someone and they tell you about their business. They tell you one of their goals is to increase sales by 20 percent over the next year.

To elicit core values, ask: "John, is success important to you?" Almost everyone answers "yes." After they say "yes," ask, "Success means different things to different people. Help me to understand, what's important about success to you?"

Their answer might have to do with taking pride in a job well done, taking care of their family, financial freedom or myriad different answers. These are their core values. If you feel you're getting more fluff than substance, you can ask for clarification. Simply ask, "Tell me more about that?"

People usually express their core value in different ways and use unique language. However, as you ask this question of a variety of people, you will gradually discover how alike we truly are. Now that you understand your customer's core values, link them together with their goals and ask the most emotionally compelling Core Values Question: "If I could show you a way that you could increase sales by 20 percent so you could have more time to spend with your family and the people you love, would we have a reason to do business together?"

This is a powerful question that shows you care. You care about their goals and their core values. You are not just trying to sell them something. You are taking an interest in helping them to enjoy the life that's important to them. That will make you highly attractive in their eyes and a person they want to do business with. It shows a willingness to do business on their terms. It's not about your goals and values or your products and services. It's about discovering their goals and core values and finding a way your product or service fits together to create a win for both of you. You are viewed as a friend who cares on a level that transcends merely business.

People find these questions fascinating. They love being asked their opinions. To them, they are the most fascinating person in the world. Ask these questions with genuine curiosity and ease, and you will be amazed at the results. When people say "Yes," it opens the door to the next "Yes," be it to an appointment or a sale. If your customer responds with, "Show me" instead of a "yes," it is still a great answer. It's an invitation to tell them more. Say, "Great! That's exactly what I'd like to do."

Some women say they feel the Core Values Questions are scripted and therefore manipulative. We speak using scripts every day; but we use them so much we forget they are scripts. When someone says, "Good morning, how are you?" and you reply, "Fine, thank you," that's a script.

Testosterone-Free Tip: The needs, goals, and core values of your clients are more important than your product or service. Use your intuition and your superior ability to form relationships, and the questions above to discover the needs of your customers and move the conversation toward doing business together.

(Discover more about eliciting core values and how it can help your business and your marketing by going to www.MarketingForHer.com, clicking on "Keyword Search" and then on "Core Values.")

The Balance of Business

If the only way to do business was slamming your fist and barking orders, it would be a sorry world indeed, wouldn't it? Most of us are unwilling to deal with people and working environments we don't enjoy.

In the entrepreneurial world, you don't have to do business with anyone you don't enjoy. There are lots of skilled, intelligent people around, so business owners often rate their friendships with vendors highly. As women, we are great at creating and maintaining positive relationships. Placing a high value on customer service will help you create repeat customers and customers who tell others about you.

Use your yin and yang qualities to become a better marketer. For example:

§ The yin energy is warm and gracious. Use a light touch with humor and a smile.

§ Your yang energy is your enthusiasm, passion, and command of a situation.

Both energies create a successful business relationship. A highly yin person may be gracious and warm but never creates an opportunity to conduct business. A highly yang person pushes too hard, too fast and turns people off. A woman with both yin and yang qualities can listen to customers *and* move the relationship towards doing business.

Connie worked for a large office supply store. Her job was going to businesses and getting orders. The office managers enjoyed Connie's visits. She was friendly and jovial, and was often the bright spot in their day. She got orders but she wasn't achieving her goals. She enjoyed her job but thought her "territory" didn't include the best businesses. She used her yin energy and did okay, but she wasn't balancing that with yang energy and projecting outward regarding new products and services.

I suggested Connie change her routine by enjoying the regular chit-chat and then asking for the business. Be straightforward. "Did you know we have great prices on printer cartridges? I'd like to be your printer cartridge supplier. Which make and model printers do your own?" Within a month, her business volume doubled. In three months, it doubled again. Connie's yin created great friendships but by incorporating the masculine energy of yang her success skyrocketed.

At the opposite end of the spectrum is the person who uses only yang energy while ignoring their yin energy. Have you ever dealt with a salesperson who never stops talking about their product or service long enough to find out about you and your needs? Or he asks questions in a pushy way so you know he doesn't care about your answers? This is super-charged yang energy. People who get only yang energy from a salesperson often conclude they are rude and pushy, and they would rather not do business with them.

You will be most successful when you balance of both the feminine and the masculine, the yin and the yang. Since most people love to talk about themselves, use your yin energy to your advantage and be a great listener. But balance it with your yang energy. Tell them the advantages of what you offer and ask for the business.

As a woman who was conditioned in ways that were not empowering to your future as a business owner, it's easy to get stuck in our yin energy without allowing our yang selves to flourish. We do not even notice when it happens. If you're going to be yang enough to own a business, you must be yang enough to project outward a bit, balancing both your feminine and masculine energy. When you squash your appropriate yang energy, your business will be less successful and you will feel anxious and less confident. (Another fascinating secret about our yin way of thinking that goes largely unnoticed can be found at www.MarketingForHer.com. Click on "Keyword Search" and then on "Make a Statement.")

Summing It Up

§ Be yourself and balance your yin and yang energies for ultimate results.

§ In business relationships with men, avoid the roles of daughter, mother, wife, or mistress that can become a minefield of problems. Be a **Sister**.

§ Men like and admire strong women but not tough women.

§ Women are perceived as trustworthy and more empathetic than men.

§ There is a delicate balance between being perceived as feminine and respected as a trusted advisor.

§ Care for your customers by dealing with them the way they want to be dealt with.

§ Ask the Core Values Questions and do business on a more personal level.

Get Started Now

- Over the next week, try the Core Values Question with at least ten people. Start with people like friends or family members. The more you practice the Core Values Questions, the more it will easily become part of you.

- The first Core Values Questions are yin. You create a relationship when you ask about their goals and values. You discover what makes them tick. The final, most important part of the Core Values Questions is yang. It's projecting outward. It's a pre-commitment question known as "a trial close."
- Tell your prospective customer what you offer and how it will benefit them. They will listen attentively because they said they would consider doing business with you. They have an emotional investment in you.
- The Core Values Questions flow directly out of relationship building.

Last Word:

Don't go eyeball-to-eyeball with men on their own turf because you generally won't win, and you'll end up feeling miserable about the interaction. Instead, try "Softly, softly, catchee monkey."

Chapter Ten

Value Yourself and Your Business Highly

"Self-esteem isn't everything; it's just that there's nothing without it"

— Gloria Steinem

Do you agonize over what to charge for your products or services? Marie, a graphic designer told me, "I just want to do my work. Why can't people pay me what they think I'm worth and leave me out of the pricing game?" That is thinking like an employee, not thinking like a business owner.

Setting prices for your services starts with your own feelings of self-worth. Marie was not confident about her worth, which made pricing difficult. You may charge much less than average for what you do because you want to "be nice," or you don't want to "sell yourself." This chapter explores why women often undercharge. It also provides an easy formula about how to determine your worth.

Pricing Is a Business Decision, not just a Personal Decision

The first time I spoke with Jan, I was delighted by her warmth and friendliness. She had a master's degree and an amazing knowledge of the Internet. She sold a package of information to help people create websites quickly and inexpensively. Jan could point web novices toward a plethora of resources so beginners could start making money online fast. She was a treasure trove of knowledge. I was convinced I had to purchase Jan's package even though she wasn't trying to sell me.

Based on my background in the seminar and info-product arena, I felt Jan's package would easily sell for $100. Jan wasn't selling nearly as many of the packages as she wanted. In fact, sales were barely a trickle. The reason had little to do with the quality of her information and more to do with how it was marketed.

Jan sent me her sales letter. I was startled to discover she was offering her package for a paltry $20. Suddenly, I didn't even want to spend $20 because it sounded cheap and second rate, and I didn't want to waste my time. "It can't be worth much," I figured. After all, people believe you get what you pay for.

Why was Jan charging so little? Because she didn't value herself. She created something that could save people countless hours. What a godsend! Yet she thought it was only worth $20. By making her package available for a pittance when similar packages were priced at more, Jan lowered her value. The result was she sold less. I told her she must increase her price. I thought her price should be five times higher, but I realized that would be out of her comfort zone. I suggested she triple her price. Quickly sales jumped upward.

If we see a highly priced item, we think it must be of high quality – especially if we are interested. This is known as "perceived value." If a high price is seen by the wrong person or in the wrong environment, the item is perceived as overpriced. Couture designer dresses are not found in Wal-Mart. When you visit an elegant boutique or fancy department store like Saks Fifth Avenue, you expect high prices. The ambience, merchandise displays, pricing, service and everything about the shopping experience work together. It's congruent. The environment of a discount store works with discount prices.

Neiman Marcus vs. K-Mart Pricing

What's the difference between a sweater found at an upscale boutique and one found in big block "superstores"? There are differences in fabric, workmanship and the way a garment is designed. However, much of the stratospheric prices are an illusion. Running advertisements in *Vogue* and *Cosmopolitan* costs a lot and keeping an image of modern opulence in front of customers is expensive.

Our spouse or partner may say aghast, "What could they possibly do to make it worth so much money?" We reply, "It's Chanel." The name explains all. That carefully crafted image comes with a hefty price tag. If you think of a white, cotton blouse as having a certain price range, it's difficult to fathom why someone might pay ten times that amount for another white, cotton blouse. However, for a person who is interested in high fashion and can afford it, the higher price tag makes sense.

To Be Viewed as Valuable, Start with Yourself

Many women don't charge enough for their products and services. Instead of being perceived as a worthy bargain, you are perceived as second rate. Unless you sell something commonly found at a discount store, it is a mistake to cut prices and be the cheapest available. When you "compete" on the basis of price, you often lose. There is always someone willing to sell more cheaply. Not only will you be undercut, you will feel discouraged. Your self-esteem will dip. The lowest priced product in a category never holds the number one spot.

Market with confidence without cutting prices. Explain the benefits of your product or service in a way that is so irresistible that potential customers will suspend their rational disbelief and buy. In pricing, as in other facets of marketing, it's important to be congruent. Your marketing message must be compelling so people who are right for your product or service will see it as the only sensible solution and happily buy.

Why Women Don't Place a High Value on What They Offer

Later I learned that Jan had been married to a physically abusive man for almost 20 years. The abuse started shortly after their honeymoon. After coaching over 1,000 people, I have learned there is a strong correlation between our self-esteem and how we value what we do for others in our business.

As women, we have a long tradition of being seen as "good" for giving away our time and effort without financial reward. Women raise children, donate their time to the PTA or volunteer at the local hospital. Men identify more with their financial achievements. That's why men experience a greater loss of identity when they lose a job. Women have a greater loss of identity when they lose a relationship.

Living with a person who tells you that you are "not enough" can have a devastating effect on your ability to value yourself. How can you value yourself after years of humiliation? I've met other women whose abusive past interfered with their ability to see their worth clearly. This degradation doesn't come from spouses alone. Parents or other family members can create a lowered sense of esteem and confidence that result in us not asking for our true worth out in the marketplace.

English writer William Thackeray said, "If a person's character is to be abused, there's no one like a relative to do it." As a result of early parental treatment, many people operate their lives out of fear. In their zeal to "protect us," family members can cause us to lower our expectations of what we can become. We cannot create financial freedom with our businesses if we are constantly struggling just to pay our bills.

The Tyranny of "Being Nice"

There are reasons women don't charge enough. Sometimes it's rooted in experiences of abuse such as with Jan above. Other times it comes from a value system that equates "being nice" with being cheap. Unfortunately it often backfires on us and we are seen as having no value or as being desperate. In fact, many women view charging the going rate as price-gouging.

Women undermine themselves by thinking:

- What will people think if I charge full price (or even charge at all)?

- I am not unique. Anyone could do what I do.
- Do I deserve it or will I be exposed as a phony?
- I should charge less because I work at home. Besides (the competition) isn't any better than me, he just has better marketing.
- People will think I'm greedy, making a living off other's problems.
- I would rather help more people and be nice than make a big profit.
- My parents taught me it's better to give than to receive.

Angie was an attorney. After becoming a mother, she decided to start a home-based practice. She shared the challenges she was having with her clients, and some clients didn't pay her after she completed work they said was satisfactory or that even exceeded their expectations. She said, "I work from home so I have less overhead. I charge half what most attorneys charge. I want to be nice. Why wouldn't people work with someone who is experienced but charges less?"

Angie didn't understand the concept of "perceived value." After all, would you feel confident going to the lowest bidder in a legal matter? Most people would feel Angie is not as capable. Her parents were hippies in the sixties and seventies, and she was raised to believe making money and wealth were bad. When she took her previous job with a big law firm, her parents were disappointed that she had "sold out" instead of helping the poor, working with Legal Aid or being a Public Defender. I asked her, "Are you attracting clients who appreciate your values of helping others, your dedication and your expertise.

"No," she sighed.

"Are you attracting clients who embrace similar values?" I asked.

"No," she admitted. "Most of them are just cheap. Often, they try to negotiate my prices downward even more. They're good at tugging my heartstrings."

I explained to Angie that, right or wrong, people judge you by what you charge. It was time for Angie to take herself seriously. She started charging full price, and immediately attracted clients who took her more seriously. She billed fewer hours yet still made the same amount of money. She had more time for family and volunteer activities.

Next, I suggested she offer her services a few hours a week to a charity she believed in. She did and connected with successful people who shared her values. Eventually she was invited to sit on the Board of Directors. People on the board started hiring Angie. She developed a reputation as a successful attorney with a heart. Her collection problems ceased and her new clients paid Angie's hourly rate. Jan and Angie didn't understand that establishing your worth as a professional is not just a business decision, but a personal one, too. It sometimes takes a lot of "inner work" to be a successful marketer.

Testosterone-Free Tip: As women, we have a tendency to minimize what we do and it's value in the marketplace. How often have you said, "Oh, it was nothing?" Your time and talents are important and valuable. Learn to say so and believe it. (To discover more about pricing and you, go to www.MarketingForHer.com, click on "Keyword Search" and then click on "The Problem with 'Being Nice.")

Pricing Secrets of Top Marketers Revealed

There is a psychology around the pricing of products and services. Marketing is about appealing to human behavior ... and that can take strange twists. A product will move at a snail's pace at $5, but when the store manager posts a sign: "Two for $9.97," the item sells out. Why does it work? Marketing experts don't always know but say, "Don't fight what works."

Odd Pricing Is a Usual Practice

When we see an item priced at $9.95, our mind plays a little trick and sees nine dollars instead of ten dollars. Not only is that a dollar less, but it's a digit less. When a high-ticket item sells for $3,995, our brains do not round up to $4,000, but rounds the price down. It's all in the eye of the beholder. Should you use odd pricing? If you want your pricing to make a statement that your product represents excellent value. Customers want to feel they are getting "a steal." Reinforce that perception by choosing an odd price point. Some things, such as professional services, don't sell well with odd pricing. People want to know you represent quality. They want you to "get it right." They don't want surprises or disappointments.

How can you keep your perceived value high while offering savings? Offer a free hour with the purchase of five or ten hours. Clients receive the paid hours first and the complimentary hour afterward. If the service you offer helps you create a result, offer a "package" and price the entire package. Sell people on the excitement of helping them completely solve their problem. Show them how you can help them get what they want. With your help, they can do it faster and easier. People don't want a process. They want a result. What is the value of helping someone achieve their dream?

The Two Most Common Pricing Strategies

There are two important pricing secrets marketers use. One is called "penetration" pricing. The second strategy is called "skim the cream" pricing.

Penetration pricing means you start with a low price with the intention of inching upward as your product develops loyal customers. This works great for products sold at retail but it presents unique challenges for service businesses. It is not wise to be cheap when delivering a service. Also, how do you raise your prices later? Many women are afraid customers will get angry and drop them. They end up feeling trapped. When you're as booked with clients as you'd like to be, it's time to raise rates. If your clients perceive you as offering a $60/hour service, some will balk when you increase your rate to $75/hour. Others will adjust to the new rates.

Price yourself fairly. Do not sell yourself short to "be nice" or avoid marketing. If you must, offer an introductory discount. Help customers understand your value by creating an emotional connection. This links to another pricing strategy known as "skim the cream."

Years ago milk was delivered to homes in glass bottles. The bottles were left on the front porch. On extra cold mornings, the cream would to rise to the top. Homemakers would pour off the cream, using it for whipped cream and other special purposes. They "skimmed the cream" off the top. It was considered the best part. *Skim the cream pricing* is where you knowingly price yourself at the top and offer luxury and status. Think Rolls Royce or Ferrari, not Ford or Volkswagen.

We have all heard of attorneys who charge $600 an hour or more. When a price point is exorbitantly high, it gets noticed. People speak in hushed tones saying, "He must be amazing. He charges twenty thousand dollars for his seminar." The crème de la crème is a man I know of who offers individual consultations for $10,000 an hour. He "reads people" through voice, body language and other visual cues, yet he has no degree as a therapist or consultant. By choosing a very high price point, you are perceived by potential customers as either extremely good or totally off your rocker. It takes courage to proclaim excellence and back it up with your price.

If you are like many women, you have found reasons to bring your prices down because you believe you're not worth as much. Jan's excuse was, "But Denise, this information is free on the Internet." She's correct. But her years of research save countless hours for her customers. Other excuses I've heard include:

§ What I offer is not the only one on the market. I'm not unique or special.

§ I haven't been in business as long.

§ I don't need to make a lot of money so I'd rather "be nice."

§ I'm not doing this full-time. It's just a hobby.

§ I would rather have more customers and be busy.

§ You have never calculated how many hours of marketing and administration it takes to do one hour of "paid work."

So how do you decide what to charge? Look at what other people in your business charge for similar products and services. How much experience do they have compared to you? How well known are they? Do you offer a unique selling feature others don't have? What unique benefit can you play up?

Taking themselves seriously and moving beyond their limited thinking made a world of difference in how the women above were perceived. Their cash flow grew significantly when their pricing was congruent with their value. Create marketing that communicates value and then increase your prices if you have been undercharging.

Summing It Up

- § Pricing is not just a business decision, but a personal decision, too.
- § Expensive goods and services are perceived as high quality if we are interested in that item.
- § The lowest-priced product in a category never holds the number one spot.
- § Communicate your value and worth rather than cutting prices.
- § Your pricing strategy should be congruent with your business image.
- § "Penetration pricing" means starting with a low price with the intention of inching the price upward.
- § "Skim the cream" pricing is where you price yourself at the top of the market.

Get Started Now

How to Determine Your Pricing for Services:

1. How much would you like to earn during the next year?
2. Divide that amount by 2,000 hours to get an average hourly rate.

3. You will have non-billable hours required for marketing and other tasks to build your business. Figure a goal of 20 hours a week in billable time.

4. Subtract the cost of overhead expenses from what you bill in a month to be left with an income that meets your needs. Overhead includes office space, utilities, marketing costs, taxes and all other business expenses.

5. Based on 80 hours of billable time per month and subtracting overhead expenses, how much do you need to charge per hour?

6. Shop your competition to determine what clients pay for similar services.

7. Use these guidelines to determine the right prices for your services.

Last Word:

It's important to your clients or customers to they feel they are in the hands of a competent professional, and one way to convey this is to charge the going market rate for your product or services. So you're really doing it for your clients' peace of mind.

Chapter Eleven

Zen Marketing and the Art of Detachment

"The only way to know how customers see your business is to look at it through their eyes."

— Daniel R. Scroggin

Do you dread picking up the phone and calling to schedule a sales meeting? Do you get tongue-tied when it comes to selling your product or service? Do you see sales and marketing as pushing, uncaring and manipulative?

The most common analogies for marketing are war, attacks, guerrillas and guns. If you have a target market, you have to shoot to hit a target, right? These analogies of war and killing used commonly in marketing are extremely yang and turn off most women. We would rather create friendship and peace.

Women generally do not regard people as targets. Are we shooting to kill or providing customers with a benefit? People who buy from me are my "focus market." I attract my customers, entice them with what they want and embrace them when they become customers. A more gentle approach, wouldn't you say?

Do It the Yin Way

Selling is about developing relationships. Capitalize on your natural yin strengths and balance them with your latent yang strengths. Selling is serving and assisting customers rather than "bagging another one." That is something hunters do with prey. Marketing is about creating. Women are excellent creators. After all, we create the entire human race.

Marketing is every activity that takes your product from conception to gestation to birth, past infancy, the terrible twos, and adolescents, and launches it into the world.

Imagine a salesperson who doesn't ask questions or care about your needs or wants. We have all encountered these annoying types of sales people, either on the phone or at your front door. No matter what you say, they do not listen or take into consideration your concerns. These are Testosterone Heavy sellers and we cannot wait to get rid of them. A smart, Testosterone-Free Marketer will listen, ask questions and make the process of buying almost effortless.

Testosterone-Free Tip: Be careful not go too far the opposite direction and assume your customers know everything about your product. Relationship-building and understanding your client needs is yin, but yin alone will not result in sales. Yang alone will not sell your products. Develop a relationship, ask questions and then ask for the sale.

A Passion for People, Not for Products

We are told we must be passionate about our business and the product or service we provide. However, Jay Abraham says, "Don't fall in love with your product. Fall in love with your customer." Loving someone means you want to know everything about them. You etch every detail in your mind and your heart. You ask questions. You start to overcome your natural fear of rejection. Flaws emerge, but when a person is known and is still accepted, that is love. Clients will be drawn to you and what you offer when you:

- See others for who they honestly are.
- Don't judge them negatively.
- Provide a valuable solution to their problem.

Because we may have felt rejected in the past, sometimes we regard prospective customers with suspicion or negativity. Take an interest in the people who are your ideal customers even before they have purchased. Zen marketing is detaching from your love for your product or service and instead falling in love with your customer.

Many people say, "If I believe in my product, I can sell it." They start a business around a product they love and are surprised when others don't embrace it with enthusiasm. Take time to understand your Ideal Customer's problems, issues and concerns. Then you can discover how your product or service will best meet their needs and serve them.

If you set your intention on something you want, you can draw it into your life. Have you taken the time to understand what your customers' needs and concerns are? Do you know your customers' characteristics and traits? What motivates them? What makes them tick? To attract clients, you must know who they truly are.

Developing Your Magnetic Focus Plan

A "Magnetic Focus Plan" will help you get a clear picture of who your ideal customers are and how you can draw them in like a powerful magnet. It can be completed easily and includes just four questions you answer more from your feminine intuition than from your thinking brain. The first two questions focus inward. They are about you and your business. The second two questions focus outward, using your Intuitive Binoculars. With each of the four questions, you quickly jot down your answers so your responses come from your core rather than spending too much time thinking about it with your left brain. When you use your Intuitive Binoculars, your answers come from the core of your knowingness that's always right if you trust it and never steers you wrong.

1. **What Will You Provide Your Customers?**

Now it is time to focus inward on what you offer. What do you want to provide your customers? Trust yourself to know what makes your heart sing. Consider your business from the point of view of something that must satisfy your wants, desires and needs to truly provide value. List all the services, products, and other items you have decided your customers can count on you to offer with confidence and passion. Only list those things you want to provide. Trust that your clarity will draw in the right customers who are a great fit for what you want to provide. Be specific. Don't just say, "I offer good customer service." Explain, in detail, what excellent customer service means to you.

2. **"How effective am I at providing those products and services?"**

Now it's time to use your Intuitive Binoculars. Take an couple minutes to bring your business into clear, sharp focus. Look at each item you wrote down in response to Question One. Ask yourself if you are effectively providing that particular service or meeting those expectations right now. Are you are providing that item or service consistently. If the answer is "No," you have an opportunity to make positive changes.

3. **Describe Your Ideal Customer**

Many business owners never get specific and know who their customers genuinely are because they put their energy and love into their product or service. When asked this question, most people respond in ways that lack clarity. Do you know the characteristics, traits and attributes of this person? If you say, "Everyone needs my product or service," then no one will. If you have never taken the time to figure out what your ideal customers are about, it's time to start. Use your Intuitive Binoculars that truly allow you to see beyond your cognitive knowing to your feminine wisdom and see your Ideal Customer. What characteristics do you discover?

Here are a few possible characteristics for your ideal customer:

- They keep their appointments.
- They trust that I have their best interests in mind.
- They look for win-win solutions.
- They are happy and effortlessly share their joy.
- They trust my intuition and my knowledge.
- They show good common sense in business decisions.
- They value a job well done.

- They pay my full fee.
- They are realistic about my time and want me to have a life.

4. **What Are Your Customers' Core Values?**

Let's bring your ideal customer into focus. Many people who market to business people consider only their customer's traits or goals, and miss out on what makes them tick. This is what motivates most people at their core. Remember the Core Values Questions from Chapter Nine? Use these questions to learn their core values. Or take a deep breath, close your eyes and use your Intuitive Binoculars to sense what you know about these people. Observe their core values closely. Write them down. Get to know your clients so well that you can tailor what you offer to them.

Now you have a four-part "Magnetic Focus Plan," including:

- What you offer your ideal customers.
- How effectively you offer it.
- The characteristics, traits and attributes of your ideal customers.
- The core values that motivate them to act.

Review your Magnetic Focus Plan or MFP daily for the next thirty days. As you focus, amazing shifts will happen if you are open. People, solutions, resources and ideas will start coming into your life, leading you to the ideal customers you want to serve.

Your Magnetic Focus Plan is a dynamic, fluid, and organic document. Consider it as cast in gelatin not cast in stone. If you want to add to it, go ahead. If you want to delete something that no longer suits you or doesn't represent your ideal customer as you consider this person more deeply, erase that item. You get to create the customers and the business that satisfies you.

The Enlightenment of Your Business

Your job is to give your customers an experience of purchasing and owning your product that makes them want to return. Your marketing should communicate the kind of experience they can count on you to provide. The questions below can help you align what you provide now with what you want doing business with you to be like:

- What feeling do you want your customers to have when they do business with you?
- Is this what doing business with you is like now?
- What impression do you want customers to have of your business?
- What are you doing to create that impression?
- Is there more you could do to create that positive experience more consistently?

Step away from your business emotionally and see what others see. Listen with an open heart and mind. This is Zen Detachment, too. You may learn something that will lead you to improve how you do business.

Scientifically conducted market research is expensive and time-consuming, but you don't have to do that. Just ask customers questions such as the ones above. Many business owners launch into a big preamble before asking a question. The more you explain before asking a question, the less likely you will get a clear, honest reply.

Frequently people ask my opinion about their book title, website or sales letter. Often they don't really want my opinion but just want to explain why they used a headline or what the title means. When prospective customers encounter it, they won't be there to explain, so it must succeed or fail on its own merits. Simply say, "I'd sure appreciate your opinion. Would you buy this or not?" Keep your questions simple.

Stay emotionally detached to the answer. People often "read into" how you ask questions. If people sense you want their approval, they probably will give it to you just to make you feel good, but it won't be an honest answer. It takes enthusiastic detachment and confidence to ask questions this way. Remember, their comments are not about you. They are just immediate feedback to your question. Stay interested but detached.

Testosterone-Free Tip: Ask people who are likely to be your ideal customers these questions. Ask the kind of people who you think would be pleased and grateful to pay for your product or service. Most importantly, make good use of the feedback you are given! (To learn more about market research, go to www.MarketingForHer.com, click on "Keyword Search" and then on "Marketing Research Tips.")

Positive Persuasion instead of Coercion

What is persuasion? Persuasion is convincing a person to change their actions or attitudes voluntarily. Coercion is changing a person through force or against their will. Many women feel that persuasion is manipulative and should be avoided, but don't we persuade our children to eat their vegetables, pick up their toys and behave politely? Don't we persuade the partner we love to love us in the way that feels warm and exciting to us? These are examples of positive persuasion, not coercion.

In marketing, the intent is to communicate information of value and help a person to adopt a new idea, product or service to their life. Marketing persuasion is about influencing people to happily say, "Yes." Through conversation and questions, you can guide your customers to tell you why they need, and are willing to pay for, the product or service you offer. Positive persuasion is about trust and opening doors. Coercion is a left-brain activity about pressure and slamming doors closed.

So, how do you positively persuade clients and customers? Dr. Robert Cialdini identified six principles of influence in his book, *Influence: The Psychology of Persuasion.* As I got to know these six principles, I made an important discovery. These principles are very balanced. Three demonstrate yin qualities and three demonstrate yang qualities. Let's explore Dr. Cialdini's six principles of influence:

1. Reciprocity: You do something nice for me and I'll do something nice for you. Doing something nice for customers puts them in a positive frame of mind. It puts them in the mood to say "Yes. This principle is definitely yin. Women are experts at giving. A mother bakes cookies for her children to see their smiles. Or, she offers to help a sick neighbor. Offering reciprocity in our marketing strategy will be second nature.

Testosterone-Free Tip: Don't give away everything free. Remember from Chapter Eight that you have value. Give a small sample of what you offer in the form of a free report, a helpful checklist or a quiz. These can be a great way to put customers in a buying mood.

2. Commitment and Consistency: Being committed and consistent makes you trustworthy. You can demonstrate this principle in the way in which you follow-up or perhaps by offering a money-back guarantee. Commitment and consistency is a yin principle. Our commitment is obvious as we interact with families, friends and the people we care about. Let your marketing show how committed and consistent you are.

3. Social Proof: Social proof says if others are doing something, that is proof of its value. Provide Social Proof through testimonials or by providing a list of satisfied customers. Social Proof is a yang principle of influence. Asking for testimonials is projecting outward. Testimonials let others brag about you. When someone compliments you on your products or services, ask if they would put that into writing as a testimonial.

4. Liking: People do business with people they like. We show we are likable by genuinely liking others first. Instead of trying to impress others, be impressed with them. Network with others and create an emotionally compelling message that shows unconditional acceptance of your customers. Liking is a yin principle. As women, we are talented at building relationships and listening.

5. Authority: Another principle of influence is to be perceived as an authority. Ways to be seen as an expert include public speaking, and authoring a book or articles. Authority is a yang principle of influence. Claiming authority is a bold, daring step that takes self-confidence. Let your yang side come out and claim your authority and expertise.

Testosterone-Free Tip: Power and authority are not given – they are assumed. Don't try to be an expert of everything. Stake your claim to your expertise in an exclusive niche. This actually makes you more credible as an expert and more powerful.

6. Scarcity: Create the impression your product or service is limited and more customers will be drawn to it. Scarcity is a yang principle of influence. Women often want to please everyone. We mistakenly believe we should have a limitless supply of our product or service. Or, we should charge as little as possible. Changing your mindset and communicating that you have a limited supply of time or a limited time offer can create more demand for what you offer.

How can you use these six principles of influence in your marketing? They are stronger and more effective when used together rather than alone utilizing both yin and yang principles. Even though influence principles like Reciprocity, Liking and Commitment and Consistency come naturally, don't shy away from the more yang influence principles including Social Proof, Authority and Scarcity.

You possess amazing strength. Consider your accomplishments. If you are a mother, when the nurse put that infant in your arms for the first time, did you imagine the obstacles you would have to overcome to raise that child? Draw upon that strength as you market your business and create the life and the financial freedom you desire.

Summing It Up

§ Marketing is about creating, not clobbering. As women, we are amazing creators.

§ Don't fall in love with your product. Instead, develop a passion for your customers.

§ Ask people who seem to be your Ideal Customers if they would buy your product or service. Market research is a valuable tool if you stay emotionally detached from the results.

§ Your Magnetic Focus Plan is the foundation of your emotionally compelling marketing message.

§ When you complete your Magnetic Focus Plan, people, resources and ideas will come to you that will lead you to the customers you want to serve.

§ Your job is to give your customers an experience of your product or service that makes them want to keep coming back.

§ Marketing persuasion is the ability to positively influence people to say "Yes."

Seek balance between yin and yang principles and activities. This balance will help you as a woman business-owner to create more cash flow and success.

Get Started Now

- List marketing strategies that are an expression of each of the six principles of influence above. Now decide to implement them in your business.
- Create a clear, compelling message that will draw in more Ideal Customers. Use words and phrases that will attract them like a magnet based on what you know about them from your Magnetic Focus Plan.
- Decide upon the best ways to get your compelling message to your customers. Look to Chapters Twelve and Thirteen for more specific marketing strategies.
- Visualize your conversations with customers going well and creating the outcome you want. Focus your attention on the other person. Smile. Studies prove we sound differently when we smile.

Last Word:

Men tend to associate more with what they do and the resulting product. Women associate more with who they are, so, they can deliver the same end result but in a more harmonious and stress-free way.

Chapter Twelve

Creating Balance and Support with Your Marketing Strategy

"Nothing in life is more exciting and rewarding than the sudden flash of insight that leaves you a changed person - not only changed, but for the better."

— Arthur Gordon

I was so excited. I was at a huge marketing seminar put on by a world famous marketing guru for entrepreneurs. I had to attend if only to find out what the fuss was about. I listened and took notes. His style was "Testosterone Heavy." No surprise there. On the second day, he wanted to describe marketing and strategy in a way that would be memorable. He asked if there was a retired military officer present. A gentleman stood up and announced he was a retired Army major. The guru asked the retired officer to explain the concept of "force multiplier effect."

"Well sir, force multiplier effect is when military forces hone in on an enemy target. We bring in all the forces to bear on one target. We bring in planes, drop bombs, and send in the tanks, helicopters and the cavalry. It all hits at once. It's pretty overwhelming and scary to the enemy on the ground. If we do it right," he chuckled, "usually the enemy crumbles and surrenders."

Then the guru said, "It's the same with marketing. When a person sees your name everywhere, after a while his or her resistance crumbles and the competition eventually gives up."

I thought, *Isn't this schizophrenic?* If we're aiming to annihilate customers on one hand while valuing them too, how can marketing be win-win? No wonder women feel they are annoying and manipulating prospective customers just by approaching them. It's time for a new way to look at marketing and marketing strategy. It's time for a new paradigm.

Come Join the Party

Imagine you receive the following invitation in the mail to a party:

> ***You Are Cordially Invited to a Grand Soiree***
> *There will be a live band with your favorite music and dancing. Your favorite foods will be served.*
> *People you enjoy talking to will be there as well as everyone you've always wanted to meet. Your presence will be appreciated.*
> *You will have the time of your life. We guarantee it.*
> *Time: Friday from 8:00 pm to Midnight*
> ***RSVP: 555-555-1234***
> PS: There will be a fee of $100 to cover all expenses

A grand soiree! Not just a party. And you love to dance, especially to live music. Plus, you are intrigued by the promises in the invitation. Everyone you ever wanted to meet will be there. Everyone will appreciate your presence. No sideways glances, no rude strangers. You look for reasons not to attend but you can't refuse. Not even when you notice the $100 fee in small letters in the lower left corner.

On Friday, you show up at the door. The home is impressive: an inviting, Victorian three-story mansion with gorgeous landscaping and comfortable wicker furniture on the porch. The door is polished oak. There is a shiny brass knocker.

Using the brass knocker, you announce your arrival. A butler graciously takes your coat and leads you to the ballroom. The room is breathtaking. Chandeliers glisten and shimmer. The décor is rich and inviting. There are fresh flowers everywhere and the scent is divine. As you enter, your arrival is announced. Everyone stops, smiles warmly and applauds your entrance.

The music from the band is your favorite and the tempo makes you want to dance. But then you spot the buffet table. You have never seen such exquisite, appetizing food. You recognize several friendly faces and immediately feel at home. Your drink order is filled by a waiter. It's delicious. Then, you recognize someone you've always wanted to meet, and he or she is introduced to you. You're enjoying a fascinating conversation and you can't believe how much fun you are having.

You eat your fill. You dance joyfully. And, you meet more fascinating, fun people in one evening than you have met in years. Time flies. Before you know it, it is midnight. Time to go home. You happily pay the $100 fee and leave a generous tip.

On your way out, you are given an invitation for next month. "Would you like invitations for your friends?" you are asked. You don't hesitate. It was worth it. You will gladly pay again! Next time you will bring a couple of friends with you because you know they will have fun, too.

That is marketing. You invite prospective customers to do business with you. The words are so enticing and appealing, they can't resist. You exceed their expectations. When you conclude your business transaction, you invite them again. Your customers are so pleased they are happy to do business with you again and tell their friends about you, too!

As women, we can throw a great party. We can make our home inviting and warm. Okay, maybe you would rather have the food catered. We can figure out what our customers or clients want and provide it. These are the yin skills of nesting, creating and nurturing. The yang, or outward projection skills, are the invitation. Yet, considering your marketing message as an invitation instead of a war makes outwardly projecting a lot easier.

Your marketing message should be like a carefully crafted invitation for potential customers and clients to join you and let you provide them with the products and services that will improve their lives. Of course, it does not have to be written like a formal invitation. It may be a sales letter, a flyer, a business card, a postcard, a website or something else. The marketing strategies you use may vary. But every time potential customers are exposed to your business, your goal is to help them feel they are being invited to something of great value. If you can do this, you will use your yin and yang skills to their full potential.

The Dining Room Table

Now that you have a new way of looking at "marketing," let's look at "marketing strategy." How can we redefine it into a more woman-friendly way than in the past?

Imagine that in your dream home is a beautiful dining room. The centerpiece is a gorgeous hand-carved table. This isn't an average dining room table. This is a dining room table big enough to include your entire family at Thanksgiving without the children sitting at a separate table. This dining room table is big enough to comfortably seat your family and maybe a few friends without anyone sitting on the sofa and perching a plate of food on their lap. In fact, if you gave an elegant dinner party for your favorite customers, it would be large enough for everyone to sit around and enjoy the lively conversation.

Visualize a table like that. The dining room is beautifully appointed and comfortably accommodates this table. Imagine you are having a big family celebration, so you begin setting the table.

First you place a beautiful, creamy linen tablecloth on the table. You top it with an antique, hand-made lace cloth that belonged to your grandmother. You set out your china. The fine silver shimmers in the chandelier's glow. The crystal wine glasses sparkle with an icy fire. Lovely fresh flowers and candles set everything off to perfection. You admire your efforts. Everything is laid out flawlessly.

The doorbell rings and guests start arriving. One by one, everyone enters your dream home in a rush of smiles, hugs and kisses. Your favorite aunt takes a silver basket of homemade rolls and places it on the edge of the table while exclaiming how beautiful everything looks. No one expects what happens next.

The table creaks with a loud groan, tips and comes crashing sideways with the weight of the basket of rolls. Your beautiful china and crystal shatters. One of the candles burns a hole in the antique lace. How did this happen?

Think back to the dining room table. When you set it, everything was set just so, but a basket of rolls sent everything toppling. The table was unstable. Upon closer examination, you discover the problem: only one skinny leg centered in the middle supported the table. All it took was one small imbalance to upset everything. When that happened, disaster struck.

Creating a Strong Marketing Table

Let's look at this story from a marketing point of view. The tabletop represents your business. The china, silver, crystal, tablecloth, and centerpieces represent the hard work, money, and pride you have put into your business and learning your skills. The one spindly leg of the table? That represents your marketing strategy.

The one leg precariously holding up the grand table top represents one marketing strategy. It could be an ezine or a website. It could be postcards mailed to a list or attending networking meetings. One marketing strategy alone isn't enough to support your business in the style you'd like. That's why we used a large table for this example. Although the whole table stayed up for a short time, it didn't last long before everything went crashing. If you only use one marketing strategy or technique and it stops working, your entire business will topple to the ground.

Let's imagine the same table with two sturdy legs. Would the table be more stable? Yes, but it would still be easy to cause the table to lose its balance and collapse. How about three legs? How about four legs? What if the grand table had eight legs? The more legs the table has, the more stable, sturdy and supported it becomes.

The same is true with your marketing. If each "leg" represents one marketing strategy or piece, as you put more strategies in place, your business becomes more sturdy and able to support you, your family and the people who work with you. If you are starting a business on a shoestring as do so many women, you are wise to get one strategy in place and working reasonably well and then begin another.

However, do not take leap to the conclusion that dozens of marketing strategies are best. Think about that beautiful table with legs packed so tightly underneath it that it resembles a solid cube. Can you push the chairs under the table? Does the table look beautiful any longer? Is it functional? Just as a table with too many legs is not useful, a business with too many marketing strategies can prove confusing. Marketing should provide leverage, not confusion. Only you can decide how big you want your business to grow. As you add legs to your strategic marketing plan, your business will grow.

Finding Your "Marketing Legs"

Marketing your business is not a one-size-fits-all enterprise. You will find your own unique path. Deciding which marketing strategies work best can be challenging, especially if you have been uncomfortable marketing in the past. Here are three simple steps to help you find what will work best for you and your product or service.

* Market only to your Ideal Customers as you defined them in Chapter Eleven. Why? They are ready and waiting to give you their business. They are the people or organizations who are most likely to buy your product. Seek out customers who will relate to you and understand your value. If you are a holistic health therapist for example, speak at the Whole Life Expo instead of the Lions Club.

* Choose marketing strategies that match your personality. Many women acknowledge they are lousy at cold calling. It just may not fit your style. Focus on marketing strategies that seem more natural and comfortable. Perhaps you would be more comfortable speaking, writing, public relations strategies and a postcard campaign. You can have a thriving business without doing things you hate. When you do things you hate, there is an incongruence that happens and you come across as not being authentic.

* Be sure you are actually marketing. Remember, it takes a balance of both yin and yang energy to be a great marketer. If you stay in your comfort zone, you may find yourself always taking courses but never implementing what you learn. You may research a business idea while someone else starts it. Or, you create business cards but are too shy to hand them out.

The Marketing Strategies for Success

Here are a few marketing strategies you can add to your marketing mix for your business. Some of these marketing strategies are discussed in greater detail in Chapter Thirteen.

Online strategies:

- Website
- Ezine or e-newsletter
- Articles on other websites to extend your reach
- Joint venture projects
- Email teasers (not to be confused with spam)
- Affiliate programs

- Search engine optimization
- Google AdWords
- Banner ads
- Online networking groups targeted to your ideal customer
- An emotionally compelling sales letter

  … and much, much more.

Here are a few offline strategies:

- Business cards
- Flyers
- Postcard mailings
- Sales letter mailings
- Networking meetings
- Public relations
- Public affairs
- Sales referral system
- Display advertising
- Classified advertising
- 800-numbers with a two-minute recording
- Television, radio or newspaper advertising
- Public speaking engagements
- Premiums (mugs, caps, pens, etc.)
- Coupon packs
- Audio tapes or CDs

  … and much, much more.

Select a few of these strategies for your business. Select ones that appeal to you. Each strategy you choose to include in your marketing mix should co-ordinate with the other strategies. For example, if you are featured on a local TV talk show, you may add to your postcards and website, "As seen on TV." If you decide to use a website, on all your offline marketing you add, "Find us on the web at . . ." and list your website URL. Dovetail all your marketing strategies so they work together as if you are adding stronger legs to the base of your table.

Plan your marketing – it doesn't just happen. The key to maintaining a marketing plan without peaks and valleys is effective planning. Some marketing strategies take more time than others to generate results. For instance, public relations can be effective at attracting ideal customers to you but it also can be time-consuming at the start. Ongoing advertising can be pre-planned. If paid advertising is one of your strategies, you may qualify for quantity discounts.

There's no hard and fast rule stating how much time you should spend marketing. If your business is new, you may need to devote the majority of your time to marketing until your business begins generating cash. Maintain a consistent marketing effort. No matter how busy your business is, continue marketing. This is especially true for women with service businesses. Many women focus all their time and energy on their current client. When "the rush" is over, they must start over and rustle up new business. It's smarter to have a waiting list of clients looking forward to your help. This keeps checks coming in steadily. It also maintains steady growth. When you're in demand, you can charge what you are worth rather than lower rates because you need a client fast. Having a few marketing legs in place supporting your table, or business, will pay big dividends.

Tracking, Tracking, 1 - 2 - 3

Developing and implementing a marketing plan is essential to success. In Chapter Fourteen, you will find an excellent way to create and fine-tune your marketing goals and strategy with your Power Pyramid. However, unless you track what you're doing, you may lose time and money.

You can increase your sales by tracking results and adjusting your marketing efforts based on the information you gather. It helps you determine what is and is not working, and it enables you to focus your efforts on the strategies that produce the most results. When tracking your marketing, remember a strategy that works for one business may not work for all businesses. There is no "set in stone" strategy that works for everyone. The marketing strategies discussed throughout this book are proven and work. You will develop your own style and technique and track your results to determine what works best for you.

Tracking means developing useful statistics that provide information about where your business is coming from. Items you may want to track include:

- How much is an individual strategy or "marketing leg" costing you?
- How much time does it take to implement?
- How many qualified leads are you getting from this marketing leg? (A qualified lead is a customer who indicates interest.)
- How many sales are you getting from this marketing leg?
- How much does a qualified lead cost you? (Total cost of this marketing leg divided by the number of leads.)
- How much does each sale cost you? (Total cost of this marketing leg divided by number of sales from this leg.)
- Is this marketing leg profitable and viable for your business?

If you gradually build an eight-leg marketing strategy and through tracking you find two strategies are not providing you with worthwhile sales, your table will be a bit less balanced but still standing. Tracking allows you to eliminate the wobbly legs and strengthen your business.

Summing It Up

§ Customers who are pleased with their interaction with you will be happy to do business with you again … and will tell their friends about you, too.

§ Your marketing message should be like a carefully crafted invitation to clients to have their needs met.

§ Each strategy in your marketing plan is another "leg" supporting your "marketing table." Choose those that best match your personality, because strategies that do not match will appear forced and unnatural … and won't be enjoyable.

§ Marketing doesn't "just happen" but is carefully planned, with your chosen strategies supporting each other like two dancers in a ballet.

§ Being independent can be "feast or famine." Keep marketing during the "feast" times to avoid any "famine" spells.

§ Track each marketing leg to learn the average cost per sale, and rank them by cost-effectiveness. Focus on those strategies with highest returns, and put the lower ranking ones on the backburner for now.

GET STARTED NOW

- How many marketing legs have you been using to stabilize and grow your business so far? Is it enough? Has it been effective?
- Do you market consistently rather than with stop and start efforts?
- Determine which marketing legs or strategies in the lists above make the most sense for your business. Choose some marketing strategies that keep working even if you do not work them. Online Internet strategies can take time to set up but work mostly on "automatic pilot" once they are started.
- Look for ways to cross-pollinate your marketing strategies. Mention your website on a flyer. Talk about an article you wrote and published in a newsletter when you announce yourself at a networking meeting. Keep looking for more ways to tell others about where they can find out more about you.
- Learn the how-tos of the marketing strategies you want to implement. Yes, there will be moments where you will feel out of your comfort zone because you must outwardly project. Use the tools in the previous chapters of this book to maintain your confidence, courage and make different conscious choices.

LAST WORD:

Choosing marketing strategies that mesh with your personality takes the "hard" out of "hard work," so that marketing can actually be fun.

Chapter Thirteen

Marketing Strategies for Small Businesses

"Marketing is not an event, but a process . . . It has a beginning, a middle, but never an end, for it is a process. You improve it, perfect it, change it, even pause it. But you never stop it completely."

— Jay Conrad Levinson

Many marketing strategies used by women-owned small businesses don't experience the success they truly deserve because they often use only yin marketing strategies, rather than a balance between yin and yang strategies. You *can* enjoy a successful business, but it helps to choose a balance of strategies for your marketing mix and invest the time and effort to make these strategies work. That means not watering down your message, but instead using a powerful, compelling message that attracts ideal customers and makes them *want* to buy now.

This chapter explores the marketing strategies briefly listed in Chapter Twelve. Here you will find a quick description of each for you to consider as part of your marketing mix. Because I am limited by paper and ink, in many cases I have referred you to more extensive information you can look to at www.MarketingForHer.com. In some instances, I have enlisted the help and support of others who are experts in one specific marketing strategy. About half of these strategies are intended to be used online and the other half are meant for bringing you and your business offline attention. Some will suit your business and/or your style and others won't. Remember, however, that in order to balance your business, you must have more than one leg under your tabletop and you must continually test to see which methods work best for you and your business.

Create a Website

Using a web site to market your business is useful when your product or service is of interest to customers who live outside of your local area. Before you decide to build a website or have one built by a web designer, it's important that you determine what you want your website to do for you and your business. Since having a website is about ecommerce, it's important to have an element of your site that's about making money or selling a product. If you offer a specialized service, your site may be simply an online brochure and an invitation for potential customers to find out more about you through a return phone call or an email. To learn more about how to select a web designer who will help you get the website you want, go to www.MarketingForHer.com and click on "Keyword Search" and then "Get the Right Web Designer."

Build an Opt-In Email List with an Ezine

Opt-in or permission-based e-mail (the terms are interchangeable) means recipients have confirmed their interest in receiving regular e-mail from you about a subject of interest. The best ezines that get marketing results are those that provide valuable content to your readers, and then occasionally offer a product or sale that you believe will be of interest to your readers. The value in ezines is that they create a trusting relationship among your readers over time through the value of the articles they provide. Ezines that are nothing but a thinly-veiled infomercial every time they are sent out soon become ignored and provide no value for the reader or the person who sends them out.

Articles Published on other Websites

Websites rely on good content to keep visitors coming back to see what's new. They are eagerly looking for writers to submit valuable articles with relevant content. When you submit an article, you are almost assured of it being published and getting visibility on their website. And the good news is that in almost all cases a link back to your website is permitted and encouraged. Clearly it makes sense to post articles only on sites where there is a possibility that your ideal customers may visit there. But since there is no cost to you in submitting articles, be generous in the sites you decide to submit articles to. For a list of websites that accept articles, go to www.MarketingForHer.com and click on "Keyword Search" and then "Article Websites."

Joint Venture Projects

Joint ventures can actually be online or offline projects. One example of a joint venture can be when you go to a website owner and see if they will be willing to give you exposure on their website for your product or service in exchange for an agreed-upon share of the proceeds for your sales. The width and breadth of joint venture projects is limited only by your creativity and your ability to communicate the benefits to another person. Joint venture projects can be a great way to extend and leverage your "reach" to those people who may be more established and already have opt-in lists of trusting customers.

Email Teasers (Not to be Confused with Spam)

Write a short, emotionally-compelling "teaser" and send it out to your email list of people who have opted-in to your list. At the bottom of the teaser, usually only two to three paragraphs in length, place a link that will take the reader to a sales offer and the opportunity to buy a product or service right then and there. Teasers work best when they are brief. Don't try to sell "The Whole Enchilada" in the teaser. Just tell them enough to "tease" them to click on the link and find out more information. The sales letter or offer provides all the information and answers all their questions.

Affiliate Programs

If you have an opt-in list of people who trust your advice and suggestions, you can make money by offering them products and services that are complementary to, and not competitive with, what you already offer. By signing up for the affiliate program of someone who offers products and services you like and are happy to endorse, you will automatically receive an affiliate commission for each sale generated from your efforts. Also, if you have a website, you can actually create an affiliate program and have other people sell your products or services online. You will need a computer programmer to develop an affiliate program for your site, or there are services available where you can actually rent the technology for your website for an affiliate program.

Search Engine Optimization

Fully 85% of people who use the Internet use search engines to find the products and services they purchase online. A whopping 90% do not look past the third page of the results list. If your site is not in the top three pages of those listings for a particular search term, your site is simply not visible to potential customers who may be looking for you. An S.E.O. specialist can help "optimize" your website, assuring that your website listing is placed in the top rankings on the search engine lists. Having your site optimized is one of the most valuable expenditures you can make in assuring that qualified traffic (ideal customers) reaches your website so that prospective clients can find out about you. To learn more about search engine optimization and how it can help your website increase traffic, go to www.MarketingForHer.com and click on "Search Engine Optimization."

Google AdWords

One of the most popular search engines on the Internet is Google.com. If you go to the website home page and/or search for information, you will see small advertisements on the right that are usually just one headline. These small AdWords ads are usually related to the search term that you asked Google to look for. Clicking on the link will take you to a website. The good news is that Google AdWords can be a great way for potential customers to find you. The bad news is that you owe money to Google every time someone clicks on the link, called a "click-through." So it's important that your headline or AdWords not just draw in traffic but draws in *qualified* traffic that is likely to convert into a paying customer. If you would like to discover more about how Google AdWords work, go to www.MarketingForHer.com and click on "Keyword Search" and then "Google AdWords Success."

Banner Advertising

Banner ads are the ads that you often see going across the top of your computer screen. They often look like a small billboard, or a square box in the left or right hand column of a website. They usually include a headline or sometimes several headlines that revolve and blink. Some internet marketing gurus believe that banner headlines are dead in terms of marketing value; however you still see them everywhere on the Internet. If a banner ad is placed in the right environment (on a website where your ideal customers are likely to be found) and the click-through price is reasonably low, it may be worthwhile to do a test to see if the banner ad results in sales. When you pay for and place a banner ad on most websites, the host will generally send you a quick report indicating how many times your ad was viewed and how many times someone clicked on it to find out more.

Online Networking Groups

Since the summer of 2003, I have been a member of an online networking group called www.Ryze.com. It includes myriad networking discussion forums where subjects range from politics to venture capital and pet care. With well over 100,000 members, there are lots of opportunities to connect with people and drum up business. Other sites that provide opportunities for networking are www.LinkedIn.com and www.Adland.com. Because these sites are very inexpensive or even free to use, many are tempted to spend a lot of time online connecting with people. But, although it can be a great resource for information, online networking is not always the highest and best use of your time unless you know the best ways to utilize these sites. To learn more about online networking sites and how to maximize their effectiveness, go to www.MarketingForHer.com and click on "Keyword Search" and then "Online Networking Effectiveness."

An Emotionally Compelling Sales Letter

Sales letters are one of the most effective ways to build cash flow online. Yes, those long sales letters you may have said you hate. Guess what? If you are willing to discover the secrets to writing a sales letter, you will increase your cash flow over and over. Most people say they object to sales letters because they just don't have time to read them. It's true; 75-80 percent of people are "skimmers," so for that reason, well-written sales letters include headlines that give the reader the gist of what it's about, whether they read the copy or not. Often those headlines draw readers and ideal customers into the copy. Besides, how many times have you said, "I hate these sales letters," and a few minutes later you were pulling out your credit card to buy something. To find out more about sales letters, go to www.MarketingForHer.com and click on "Keyword Search" and then "Money-Making Sales Letters."

Offline Marketing Strategies

In our quest to optimize all the strategies available on the Internet, sometimes we forget offline marketing strategies are still an effective way to attract ideal customers to you. In fact, some marketing experts argue that offline strategies are more effective than ever because in the pell-mell race to get online, there isn't nearly as much "competition" for the eyes and ears of your customers offline. Have you noticed that while you may still have as many bills in your mailbox, there are fewer postcards, sales letters and other offline marketing efforts used? I would be remiss if I did not address some offline strategies that many home-based business owners on a shoestring budget have found effective.

Business Cards

Never go anywhere without your business cards in tow. Be sure to slip a few in your purse every time you leave the house, just as you would make sure you have a pen, cash and lipstick in your purse. Your business cards should reflect you and the business you are creating. Make sure that your business card includes all the pertinent contact information, as well as a tagline that sums up the unique difference that your business brings to its ideal customers. Generally I do not recommend business cards that are printed on vividly colored card stock. Often they are difficult to read, especially for people over 40. Some business owners choose a fold-over card that gives you the option to create an entire mini-brochure with your card. While business cards may not seem "sexy" in our fast-paced, wireless world, studies show that people see business cards as having value and that people tend to keep them.

Flyers

Flyers are the stock-in-trade of many who are just getting started in business and need something fast and inexpensive to get the word out about what they do. Remember to write all your written copy from the viewpoint of your ideal customer. This means that you tell less about the product or service or about you, and more about the benefits to the client of what you're offering. For optimum legibility, print flyers in black ink on goldenrod yellow paper, for it seems to "pop" the best. As you're writing your flyer, make sure that you come up with an attention-grabbing headline that will make people want to read more. There is a huge difference in results between an ad or flyer with a great headline and a merely so-so headline, so time spent in this area is time well spent. Be sure that you also include all the necessary contact information on your flyer so that people will know how to follow up and inquire for more information or buy your product or service.

Postcard Mailings

These little gems can pack a marketing wallop and bring customers to your website or call you on the phone for more information. You don't see a postcard individually in your mailbox these days. Some companies coordinate into packets postcards from a number of vendors who may be interested in the same kind of ideal customers. The same company can also arrange inexpensive mass 4-color printing. An important issue with postcards packets is geographic reach. You want to make sure that your postcards go where you can do business. If you offer services only in your local area, it makes little sense to purchase space in a postcard packet mailing that goes out nationwide. Learn how to write compelling bullets, i.e., quick benefit statements that will help the reader to say, "Yes, that's me. That's what I need." If you can do that, they will want to follow up at your website or by placing a phone call to you.

Sales Letters via Direct Mail

En masse, a direct-mail sales letter can be prohibitively expensive for a home-based business owner. However, when used with a small list that is niched to business customers and followed up with a phone call, a sales letter can be a highly effective way to tell people about your business-oriented product or service. However, with business customers, you cannot ramble on and on. Generally speaking, two to four pages is the maximum length for a sales letter. Consumer companies such as credit cards, travel offers and subscription offers still use direct mailing with great success. I know small business owners who go through their local Chamber of Commerce list and focus on those businesses that seem like the best fit, perhaps sending out less than fifty letters a week. In one instance, I suggested that a woman who was a virtual assistant send out only twenty letters a week. I did not want her sending out any more letters than she was willing to follow up with on the phone. Every time she sent out one of these micro mailings, she got new business. Within two months, she had enough business lined up to keep her busy with clients for the foreseeable future, so she stopped sending the letters

Networking Meetings

Most business owners agree that networking meetings can be highly valuable but that it is not the short route to sales and making your cash register ring. Networking works when you have a flair for the creative. When you meet someone, don't think, "Is this person a possible customer for what I offer?" That's how most people at networking meetings limit their opportunities. Instead think, "Is there a way we could possibly work together to help each other out?" When you put this "win-win spin" on your networking activities, you actually use leverage. You will get a different kind of results that lead to more business and cash flow. One of the most important things to remember with networking is to follow up with people. If you get a business card and you have an idea, be sure to pick up the phone and call to move the idea forward and manifest great results for both of you.

Public Relations

Did you know that business owners actually use the media to get the word out about their businesses? It's called public relations and it used to be exclusively the purview of large corporations until smaller businesses started finding out the benefits of getting exposure in the media. Amazingly 70 percent of the news headlines you read are generated through public relations. You send a one-page article known as a media release off to your local newspaper or other media outlet and then watch the headlines appear and your sales increase. Clearly there is a lot more to public relations, or PR as it is known, than just sending off any old article. However, the benefit of PR is that articles written about you are free in the newspaper as opposed to paid advertising. Also, an independently written article has more of a ring of truth and credibility than does a paid advertisement. To learn how you can use public relations, go to www.MarketingForHer.com and click on "Keyword Search" and then "Public Relations Bonanza."

Public Affairs

Getting involved in your community puts you in the public spotlight, and being noticed brings you new business. For example, you could volunteer your time to an organization allied to your field, such as the local Chamber of Commerce. And most cities have ongoing education programs, often run by the Parks and Recreation Department, so you could offer to teach a class in your field of expertise. (Recall from Chapter 4 how Bethany offered a workshop at her gym.)

One independent computer consultant I know wrote so many media releases to local newspapers and TV stations that he became known as an expert on the subject. When a news item broke involving computers, newspaper editors and TV news producers would call him up for his "expert commentary." This brought the consultant exposure and credibility. Is there a subject area in which you could become known as the local expert?

Sales Referral System

The easiest way to get new customers is to get satisfied old customers to bring you new business. Most people simply pray and hope to get referrals but you can actually create a flow of referrals by developing a referral system or incentive program that encourages people to bring new customers to you. Depending on what business you're in, some people think that being "paid" for a referral is somehow crass or dishonest. Other people love it. The best way to determine what kind of incentive you might consider offering is to ask a few of your favorite customers. Other possible offerings you might provide to encourage referrals can include a discount on future products and services, a donation to a local charity, an introduction to someone they would like to meet, a free advertisement a laudatory article in your ezine or website, or anything you can come up to thank your customers for sending you customers.

Display Advertising

I have often made a joke that display advertising is "the black hole of marketing," because lots of money goes in but nothing seems to come out. Of course, they do work, especially for high-end, image-intensive products such as perfumes and luxury cars. (The next time you read your favorite magazine, count the proportion of pages carrying advertising compared with actual content.)

Because of the high cost, display ads require particular care:

- Thoroughly research your target market. If you've written a book, are you aiming at retail buyers to come to your website, or at bookstore owners to carry your book on their shelves? If you're a CPA, are you targeting individuals or small businesses? Of if you sell animal care products, is your target pet-owners or veterinarians?

- Once you know your target, research what they read. There are literally thousands of magazines out there catering to an infinite number of special interests, collectors, hobbyists, and so on.

- Once you narrow down possible media, get hold of their advertising rate sheets, and work out how much space you can afford to buy.

- Next, craft the invitation. Present your product or service in terms of meeting the needs of *readers*, and not your need to get their business. Will your product or service make them richer, sexier, thinner, healthier, happier, better informed? Study Maslow's Hierarchy of Needs—even after 50 years, it's still relevant because human needs don't change all that quickly. (A Google search yields about 9,000 pages on the subject if you're not familiar with it.)
- Once you know *what* you want to say, hire a graphic designer or learn graphic design yourself, but learn the computer software well, because it's an expensive way to show the world you're a neophyte. Of course, graphic design is a *huge* subject, too large to cover here.

Unless readers must write or call you to order, this is a hard strategy to track, akin to blindly firing a shotgun, hoping to hit something.

Classified Advertising

Carefully worded classified ads, well-placed in the monthly magazines and daily newspapers that potential clients read can be an inexpensive way to reach them, especially with multiple insertions. Of course, they are inexpensive because not everyone reads the Classifieds, so do not expect a high return. Remember to include a tracking code so that you can monitor the success or otherwise of the various media you use, and which months of the year or days of the week bring the best response. (Newspapers recommend Friday and Sunday as the hottest days for Classifieds.)

800-Number with a Two-Minute Recording

A recording on an 800-number can be economical because you pay only for the calls received. This form of exposure has a number of benefits:

- You can change the message at any time to reflect changes in product availability or price.
- You can emphasize any special offers you're running.
- Callers feel closer to you because they can hear your voice.

When making your recording, use the same techniques as when recording your outgoing answering service message: write it out, rehearse several times, SMILE as you read it, sound upbeat and enthusiastic but not breathless, speak slightly faster than normal conversation, and most importantly, replay it, listening carefully.

For example, an astrology service offers a free generic daily forecast as a tease to stay on the line and be switched to a pay-by-the-minute 900-number forecast for the caller's specific sunsign.

TV, Radio or Newspaper Advertising

Unless you're in the big leagues, you'll probably be aiming at local markets, but everything that applies to Display Advertising applies here, too. Who is your target, and what channels, stations and newspapers to they go to? How much space or airtime can you afford to buy? And how much can you spend on production? For TV, stills are boring but inexpensive, compared with the cost of shooting on location, especially if you use professional actors. For radio, conversations between two friends are a popular format for "discussing" your product or service.

A cheap way to buy airtime is on a contingency basis, where the station drops your commercial into an otherwise empty slot. Of course, that slot may be at three in the morning, but you get it for pennies on the dollar.

Newspaper advertising follows the rules of the Display Ad strategy, but remember that in any written medium, poor grammar and spelling errors will severely damage your credibility, so make sure you have the piece checked by someone else, preferably a professional editor. And watch for unintended double meanings. A medical clinic ad headlined: "Want to get pregnant? Dr. John Smith is at your service" will generate more amusement than clients. Your single-minded focus on what you want to say may blind you to other meanings that can be read into something.

Public Speaking Engagements

A recent survey poll showed that, for most people, fear of public speaking completely swamps fear of death, but if you *can* get up on your hind legs and address a gathering, this is one of the most cost-effective strategies of all.

If you would rather stick needles in your eyes than climb up on a podium, there are countless ways to overcome your fear, from hypnosis to visualizing your audience naked (unless you're the keynote speaker at your local nudist club). Just remember three things:

1. You're the expert and know more than most of your audience does about your topic.
2. They want to be entertained as well as informed, so keep your sense of humor. (Remember me tripping on the steps up to the podium.) In one presentation, when the whiteboard and easel crashed to the floor, the speaker didn't miss a beat: "Now that I have your attention, ladies and gentlemen …"

3. Most people are good-at-heart and really *want* you to succeed, so will more than meet you halfway.

Research upcoming gatherings of professional groups and associations in your field, and contact the speaker coordinator to arrange a slot for you. Initially, you may need to pay your own way, but once you're recognized, expenses should be handled for you, along with a sizeable honorarium.

Talk Radio

An extension of the previous strategy is to be interviewed as a guest on talk radio. Hundreds of radio stations nationwide with thousands of hours of programming to fill means unlimited opportunities for interesting people with interesting things to say.

You can purchase lists of radio stations, with the names and numbers of hosts and producers, and target them with your faxed or emailed press release, telling them why you would make an excellent guest on their show. And back it up with a list of questions that the host can ask you on the air. This is invaluable, as it makes the host appear intelligent and in touch with the subject, and feeds you with exactly what you need to make your points.

Remember that radio stations stay in business by selling ad time, where the rates are set by their share of listeners, so the more controversial and *avant garde* you are, the more listeners the station retains, which guarantees you will be called back. However, when the program "goes to the phones," be prepared for just about anything. Callers will attack you and your ideas, so rehearse beforehand with a friend who is willing to play devil's advocate and give you a thorough workout.

The best part of talk radio? It's all done by phone from your kitchen table, with you in your robe, sipping your morning coffee.

Premium Items

Mugs, caps, pens, calendars, T-shirts, refrigerator magnets, paperweights—the list is endless. And so is the list of companies that will put your name and logo on them at surprisingly little cost. The main benefit is that, unlike a newspaper that's tossed after a quick read, this exposure keeps on selling every time someone looks at or uses the item.

Again, research your market and, for maximum exposure, what they would find *really* useful. As always, your marketing budget will determine how upscale you can go but here, cost and exposure don't always go together—an accountant will see your name a hundred times a day on a $5 calculator.

Coupon Packs

A popular strategy to get exposure is to buy into a coupon pack, either nationally or locally. Use your slot to offer a discount (possibly with a time limit or dollar minimum), a two-for-one special, or some other enticement. The coupons can be postcards in a mailer, perforated tear-outs in the phone book or "Welcome to the Neighborhood" package, or any other way to reach your target market.

Apart from the initial insertion cost, this strategy only costs you money when clients or customers redeem the coupon, which is a great time to cross-sell your other products or services.

Audio Tapes and CDs

Cassette tapes and CDs are cost-effective marketing tools. In creating them, consider the same issues as for 800-number messages: plan your content, write your script, rehearse, record and replay.

For decades, books on tape have been popular with people on the move. Likewise, you could record your own tapes, where you offer valuable advice in the area of your expertise, interspersed, of course, with your sales message. This is low stress marketing for you and your clients, and offers a valuable service, too. However, the last decade has seen a whole new technology come along.

In supermarket chains across the country, Internet giant America Online has display racks of its free installation CD-ROM. And for a small outlay, you too can harness this remarkable marketing strategy. Once an audio studio has burned your content onto a master disk, they can quickly make copies for a few pennies each. (Of course, you can do it yourself on any modern computer, but each disk takes a few minutes of your precious time.) Then all potential customers need to do is pop the CD into their computer and Autoplay brings up the first screen of information.

Businesses can showcase their offerings using animation, hot jumps within the CD, and hot links to their Internet site. Content is limited only by the designer's imagination and your budget. For example, realtors could present a photo-tour and floor plans for each property they represent, and hand out CDs to potential buyers and other realtors. As always, the trick is to get the CDs into the hands of qualified buyers. For a few more dollars, a realtor could offer a video walkthrough of the home on a DVD as well as via streaming video through their Internet site. This allows buyers in distant cities to make their decision without even leaving home.

Some small publishers create a CD-ROM with the book cover and excerpts for each of their literary offerings, along with audio interviews with the authors, plus a hot link to the publisher's website so that people can immediately buy books online. And the enormous capacity of a CD-ROM means that several small publishers could collaborate on one cooperative CD, with cost savings for everyone. Once DVD burners are commonplace, they could even include video clips, too.

Thanks to today's computer ownership, every potential client already has the necessary viewing device, so along with the ever-burgeoning Internet, this could well be the basis of the newest marketing strategy … and very cost-effective, too.

Summing It Up

§ There are dozens of strategies you can use for testosterone-free marketing, avoiding the in-your-face tactics favored by the males of our species

§ Developments in Internet and computer technology offer ever-new more powerful techniques to reach potential customers or clients, as well as the "tried and true" methods.

§ Strive for a balance in strategies that matches who you are with the size of your marketing budget.

Getting Started Now

- Out of the almost 30 marketing strategies in this chapter, select a half dozen or so, and commit to using them in the next three to six months.
- Prepare a written plan, with landmark dates and measurable goals, such as "By June 1, be a guest on three talk radio shows," or "Mail out three press releases to local media."
- Track the sources of sales or consulting assignments, tying them back to your use of specfic marketing strategies.

Chapter Fourteen

Your Power Pyramid for Success

"To accomplish great things, we must not only act, but also dream; not only plan, but also believe".

— Anatole France

Even though you are one of the lucky women who have a dream, you must decide how to achieve your success. You need a plan to help you determine how to get what you want.

I've provided you with:

- A clear understanding of why you have held back in the past from marketing.
- Ideas to help you get beyond your obstacles.

- A new marketing paradigm that is more woman-friendly.
- Knowledge that will help you create a business resulting in financial freedom instead of just another job.
- Marketing strategies that can help you be more successful.

In this chapter is a tool I call Your Pyramid Plan for Success. Your plan will help you eliminate remaining feelings of overwhelm. The steps to achieve your goals will become clear. You will start attaining the results and freedom you want. Your Pyramid Plan is like a diagram for success. This system provides you with the inner knowing and motivation to achieve the success that has eluded you. You will see more clearly what needs to be done, especially in those areas outside your comfort zone.

Your Power Pyramid Plan for Success will include your:

- S.M.A.R.T. Goal
- Undeniable Purpose
- Clear Compelling Vision
- Guiding Principles
- Action Strategy
- Agenda Items
- To-Dos
- Personal Support System
- Personality Traits that Work in My Favor
- Personality Traits I May Choose to Shift
- Rewards for Achievement
- Statistics for Your Success
- Affirmations to Guide You
- Commitment Statement.

Each step you complete will help you get more excited. As your Pyramid Plan takes shape, you will know you can turn your dreams into your reality.

Make Your Goals S.M.A.R.T. and Purposeful

Goals create a diagram from which to work. A goal is clear, succinct statement of your intention. A goal is something you intend upon being, doing, or having. It's wise to set S.M.A.R.T. goals. That means your goals are:

1. **S**pecific
2. **M**easurable
3. **A**chievable
4. **R**isky (a stretch for you)
5. **T**ime-bound (set a deadline for yourself)

Let's define each of these five components to your S.M.A.R.T. goal:

Specific means your goal is clearly defined. It has boundaries and it's apparent when you've achieved it. Goals that are not specific can become negative because you have no idea when you're done.

Measurable. Without measurable goals, it's difficult to determine if you've succeeded or not. How do you know when you have arrived? Numbers are an easy way to make a goal measurable. If you set a goal to improve a relationship with a client, perhaps you can make it measurable by saying, "I will call weekly to check if there are any customer service issues to be addressed."

Achievable means there is a possibility your goal can be achieved. If you have never studied medicine, it's unrealistic to think that you will become a surgeon in the next year. Amazing things can happen but your goal should be within the realm of possibility.

Risky means the goal is a stretch for you. Small, goals with no challenge don't attract us or draw us in. Big goals that make you draw your breath in sharply are the ones that make you passionate and spur you on to greater success. These are risky goals.

Time-bound means you have a deadline for completion.

- Short-range goals are generally 30, 60, 90 or 120 days.
- Medium range goals are six months to two years in duration.
- Long range goals are thought of as two or more years.

For your first S.M.A.R.T. Goal, choose a short-term goal. Write down your goal in one or two sentences. You don't have to know how to achieve your goal; just know that it is what you want to accomplish. Write down your S.M.A.R.T. goal. Do it now.

Your Undeniable Purpose – The Power behind Your Goal

Your Undeniable Purpose is the driving force behind your goal. If you do not have a big enough "why," you will never find the "how." These are the reasons deep inside you that compel you to keep going until you achieve your goal.

It's not enough to say Your Undeniable Purpose is "to create income." Dig deeper. How will this income align with your core values? Will you send your children to a private school? Take an exotic vacation? Hire a trainer and run a marathon? What will inspire you to stay the course? Your Undeniable Purpose gives your goal the push you need.

Write Your Undeniable Purpose – the "why" of your goal. When you look at your purpose, it will nudge you forward. Sit down and write your purpose for your goal. Don't skip it. Beneath your S.M.A.R.T. Goal, write, "My Undeniable Purpose is …"

The Power of Visualization

Without a vision nothing happens. When you visualize yourself succeeding, you can see the light at the end of the tunnel. Visualize the feelings you will enjoy when your goals are achieved. You will realize how important your goal is to your happiness and success. For your Power Pyramid, you will visualize in a conscious, aware way. In Chapter Seven, you wrote out a long-range Clear Compelling Vision. Sometimes it seems so far from view that it's difficult to connect with your vision in its completed form. Write out how you will feel when you have achieved your short term 30- to 120-day goal.

Visioning your goal in its completed form is a powerful tool that can propel you toward the abundant future you want, rather than keep you stuck. Your path to success becomes so real you can almost feel it, hear it, smell it, as well as see it.

Write your shorter-range Clear Compelling Vision as if you are writing from the future. Write as if you have achieved your S.M.A.R.T. Goal. If you set a 90-day goal, write as if it is 90 days from today, and you're look back to today, as if you are reminiscing about when you set the goal. Now that you've accomplished your goal, describe how you feel. Write how you felt about setting this goal and how you've changed or grown as a result.

Don't say, "I will feel more knowledgeable and confident." That is how we talk about the future. Instead say, "I feel more knowledgeable. My confidence has soared." Write about the positive changes that have occurred as a result. Do you feel differently about yourself? Are you planning a vacation? Has your business revenue increased?

Your Clear Compelling Vision is like a dialogue with you as the star of a movie, describing the pleasure you feel of having reached your goal. Describe it in full sensory detail. What do you see, smell, taste, hear and feel? Without a Clear Compelling Vision, you won't be able to see what you're working for. You may not be satisfied with what you have in your life now. However, your subconscious mind tends to keep us where we are, so your vision will make it easier to create that change with ease.

Take five minutes to write your Vision. Give your 30- to 120-day S.M.A.R.T. Goal energy, power and clarity. Close your eyes and visualize what you are doing, thinking and feeling once your goal has been achieved. Don't deny yourself the pleasure of a Clear Compelling Vision that will help pull your S.M.A.R.T. goal into reality.

Your Guiding Principles

Guiding Principles are guidelines by which you and others will operate. Your Guiding Principles will help you make decisions effortlessly. All you need to do is check in and determine whether or not a decision is in alignment with your Guiding Principles.

Your Guiding Principles will help you determine which direction you want to go as problems and opportunities arise. Below is a list of Guiding Principles I have used. This list may inspire you to develop your own list of Guiding Principles.

- Do business with integrity and honesty.
- Under-promise and over-deliver.
- Start with the end in mind.

- Return phone calls in 24 hours.
- Offer a strong guarantee for customers.
- Do not take on more than I can handle.
- Spend time in the highest and best way possible.

Write out the Guiding Principles you want to include for your S.M.A.R.T. Goal. Work with them for a while. As time goes on, you may decide to apply some of them to your entire business.

From Action Strategy to Agenda Item

An Action Strategy is a wide area of activity essential to accomplish your S.M.A.R.T. Goal. Your Goal may include one or more Action Strategies. Each Action Strategy is written in one sentence. Write down the major Action Strategies necessary to complete your S.M.A.R.T. Goal. Do it now. Your goal will start to become more concrete. For example, if your goal is to have your website up and running in the next sixty days, your Action Strategies might include:

1. Hire a web designer and discuss approach, site style, etc.
2. Create relationships with people who want to sell their products on your website so you have a site with a money-making component.
3. Write the marketing copy or content for your website
4. Have traffic optimized through search engine optimization or other methods
5. Review and sign off on designer's final work product
6. Monitor traffic to site.

The next part of your Pyramid Plan is your Agenda Items. Agenda Items include shorter-range steps essential to complete an Action Strategy. As you break your Action Strategy into smaller steps you will feel empowered and see clearly the path to reach your goal. You will understand why your goals and dreams have gone unfulfilled in the past.

Using the example above, if one of your Action Strategies above is "Hire a web designer," your Agenda Items to reaching that goal might include:

1. Get referrals to web designers from friends
2. Make sure you are both clear on the work to be completed
3. Talk with them and have them submit proposals
4. Review proposals and make a decision on which web designer is best for your needs.
5. Identify interim work products and delivery schedule
6. Review and critique/approve interim work products as delivered

If you reach a point where you don't know what should go in your Agenda Items, you may feel uncomfortable because you don't know what to do next. Ask, "What people, resources and information will help me find the answers so I can keep moving forward?" Asking questions is a great way to learn. What you don't know becomes clear and is no longer a dark, gray cloud of overwhelm. It's merely a question. Questions can guide you toward the people, resources and information you need. Each question leads you to more clarity and solutions.

To-dos and the Tyranny of the To-Do List

The last level of your Pyramid Plan is "To-dos." They are those little items we love to check off every day from our list. They are items delegated to yourself or others. To-Dos are suggested for your convenience. The important thing is to build your Pyramid Plan to suit YOUR needs, so it makes sense for you. Don't break your goals down to the point of silliness – "Pick up the pencil" for example. Think of as many details as you can. If you don't know how to complete a task, write down questions that will help you get closer to the answer.

A To-do List can be overwhelming because there can be so many items depending on the size of your goal. It can appear daunting. Where do you start? Once you have a To-do list, start setting priorities. Number your To-Dos in the order you believe they should be completed. If you don't know what order your To-Dos should come in ask more questions. Look for the people and resources that can help you discover answers. (If you're short-term S.M.A.R.T. Goal has to do with a marketing strategy, you may find help at www.MarketingforHer.com. Click on "Keyword Search" and then "S.M.A.R.T. Goals.")

Completing easy tasks can provide an emotional boost. Best-selling author Robert Allen calls this "the tyranny of the To-Do list." Finish the big items in your Pyramid Plan that move you forward the most rather than small To-Dos that keep you in your comfort zone. Allen suggests, "Do your feared thing first." Complete the two or three items that are most important when your energy is high. Don't put menial items at the top of your list.

It's not important how many items you cross of your list but that you cross off the most important items. This will increase your confidence. Think courageously as you choose which items come first, second, third, etc. Setting priorities is an important part of being a business owner, and will help you feel less overwhelmed and more clear.

Enlist Your Support Team

We all need support. Who are the people in your life who are unconditionally loving and supportive? Maybe it's your family. Maybe not. What about that person who always asks about your business and has great ideas? How about that friend you have coffee with who always has positive suggestions? Who can you call on, talk to and open up with?

Make a short list of the people you can call on when times get rough or simply thinking about them brightens your day. Who has knowledge you can tap into on topics you know little about? Who might be able to refer you to someone who would be of help?

None of us can do everything alone. Yet women often believe if we don't do it alone, we can't take credit. Don't be overly independent. You deserve help and support. In the home-based business world, there are no glass ceilings but few mentors either. (For tips on creating a great mentoring relationship, go to:

www.MarketingforHer.com, click on "Keyword Search" and then "Great Mentoring Relationship.")

Affirm What You Want

Don't forget to be supportive of yourself. One way to take good care of yourself is to consciously monitor what you say to yourself. Make sure you're feeding yourself positive, powerful messages. A good way to do this is by using affirmations. Powerful affirmations can support and guide you. An affirmation can be a statement of a truth you have not embraced yet. Start your affirmations with "I" and write them as if your goal has already been achieved. Write at least two affirmations that will help you overcome potential obstacles to completing your S.M.A.R.T. Goal. (For a list of great affirmations, go to www.MarketingforHer.com, click on "Keyword Search" and then "Affirmations." Repeat your affirmations for at least 21 days to help you stay on track with your goals.

Make a Commitment to You

By making a commitment to yourself, you are stating the gravity of your intention. When you write your Commitment Statement and sign and date it – powerful, unseen forces work in your favor. Take a few minutes to write a Commitment Statement to yourself. Start with "My commitment to myself is to …" Your commitment to yourself need only be a couple lines in length. (For an example of a Commitment Statement that I have used for some of my Power Pyramid goals, go to www.MarketingforHer.com, click on "Keyword Search" and then "Commitment Statement.")

What Qualities Work in Your Favor?

What qualities do you possess that will be an asset as you bring your S.M.A.R.T. Goal to fruition? Assess your strengths. We possess wonderful qualities that we take for granted. Make a list of the strengths you bring to your 30- to 120-day goal. Use your strengths if times get rough. They will propel you towards the achievement of your goal even faster.

There are some personality traits it may be helpful for you to strengthen. Most of us put time and energy into improving where we already excel. For example, if you are family-oriented, perhaps you have a happy family life but you have not put time into developing the financial side of your life. You might be a wonderful giver but you need to develop your receiving muscles. Perhaps you are shy and it would be helpful to be more outgoing. If you are spontaneous, it might be helpful to develop more discipline. Respond with new conscious choices when your tendency is for old behaviors to click into place. Remember, *Testosterone Free Marketing* is about responding with new conscious choices that work rather than old knee-jerk reactions.

Don't Forget to Reward Yourself

How will you acknowledge yourself for successfully completing your S.M.A.R.T. Goal? You deserve to savor your achievement. Do something special, otherwise life becomes one goal running into another without any rewards along the way. So stop, breathe deeply, and say, "Wow! I did it!" Your reward can be a massage at a spa, a weekend getaway or fresh flowers in your office. You decide. Write down your reward right now.

Make Your Pyramid Plan "Congruent"

As you create your own Pyramid Plan for Success, each component must be in alignment with every other part. Develop a plan that works with your life. Read it from the top down and read it again from the bottom up. It is congruent? Does it still make sense? This important step will provide you with a clear road map to the success you deserve.

Statistically Speaking . . .

Did you know statistics can be exciting? Statistics are measurements used to chart your progress. They provide a quick check of how you're doing. Valuable statistics include:

- § Revenue
- § Increase in Revenue
- § Number of customers
- § Number of new customers
- § Number of sales
- § Dollar amount per sale
- § Number of items per sale
- § Profits
- § Number of pages written in your book.

Decide which statistics to track. There are times when you feel things are not progressing as you would like, but when you look at the statistics you can see growth. Or, you may think your business is doing well, but you wonder where all the money goes. Statistics will give you an accurate benchmark of where your business is going.

Summing It Up

· Your own Power Pyramid will help you create a road map. Chunking down your goal will make your goal feel less daunting and more achievable.

- When you don't know what to do next, start asking questions. Questions make our challenges seem more manageable.

- Asking for help and mentoring does not make you any less independent.
- Your Clear Compelling Vision will inspire you toward the business you want to create. It will bring you closer to what you want and deserve.

Get Started Now

Keep in mind you can use the Pyramid Plan structure for any goal. From a business or marketing goal to losing weight or finding your soulmate, the steps in this chapter will help you achieve your S.M.A.R.T. Goal. Make sure you implement your plan.

Last Word:

Driving the full 3,000 miles from New York to San Francisco can seem a daunting task, but if you break the 60 hours drive time into six 10-hour days, the task becomes more doable.

Chapter 15

About the Man in Your Life

"Love is the selfless promotion of the growth of the other."

— Milton Mayeroff

I wrote this entire book and was rejoicing at its completion when several of my gentleman friends said, "Don't forget the men. You need at least one chapter in your book to help men understand the women we care about and appreciate."

So I went back and asked them, "What would be helpful for you? What do you want to know?"

I got a few lame replies and even more blank stares in return.

My friend Sue, who is clever and sensible in all matters gender-wise, told me, "It's not because men don't care. It's because they don't know what they want. They are looking to us to tell them what we need – not the other way around. I think it's more a question of what women want … and want men to know."

So, I asked women, "What do you need from your partner to feel supported and appreciated? What do you need them to do and say?" The responses poured in.

Many of us enter relationships thinking that now we're in love, the other person will complete us and meet all our needs. Both men and women tend to think like this. It may feel that way at first but as a member of a couple we are separate, distinct individuals. And while most couples have common goals, such as owning a home or having children, we also often have individual goals that are important to us, too.

The Green-Eyed Sabotage Monster

Women sometimes tell me their partners behave in ways that lack confidence toward them. They do things to dis-empower the woman they say they love rather than encourage her to be her best. Sometimes, without even realizing it, we can sabotage each others' efforts. This is the opposite of unconditional love and support. Have you ever gone on a diet and your partner brought home ice cream? That's an example of relationship sabotage. Has he ever come home all excited about a new idea and you told him it will never work? That can be another form of sabotage.

If a man expects a woman to be his adoring, subservient "love slave" 24/7, he's insecure. Consider powerful men who changed the world or the way we think for the better. Or perhaps there's a local man who changed your community for the better. Those men had a bigger vision and game of life to play than worrying and fretting if "the little woman" was home waiting for them every minute. Their drive to express what they were passionate about kept them moving forward.

People undermine another person's efforts out of feelings of insecurity and lack. Those are feelings of, "I'm not enough." What happens when a man does things to undermine his partner's business? He is obviously threatened. The question is, "Why?"

If your partner is constantly worried about keeping you "under his thumb," it's time for him to develop more self-confidence. Command and control may work in sports or war but they do not work in lasting, loving relationships.

Mary, a highly esteemed freelance writer, said, "My husband used to resent it when, in his opinion, I spent too much time on my business. Yet, he basically ignores us and does his own thing most of the time. He's the kind of personality who needs a lot of 'cave time.' Yet, he has always expected me to drop what I'm doing and be with him when he wants. It's unfair, but I don't pay it any mind anymore.

The point of dissention here is not that the husband is not supporting his wife. The crux of the problem is he no longer feels he is the center of her life. He must have felt this way at one point to feel the loss of that importance now. That defined him. He needs that kind of validation. "Being the center of the family makes him 'feel like a man,' " says Mary.

Sabotage starts in subtle ways. Women, being the nurturing creatures we are, don't always see it when the demands become overwhelming. As a woman in a relationship, we have a responsibility to do what it takes to be happy for ourselves and know what we want. The dichotomy is that as little girls we were trained not to ask for what we want. Most of us were trained that we are "good little girls" when we put our own happiness on hold and are self-sacrificing. When you become consciously aware of what makes you tick and what your dreams and visions are, you have a responsibility to communicate that to your partner.

If your partner loves you and wants good things for you, chances are he is waiting for you to clearly tell him what you want. However, sometimes women play games. We believe lies like, "If I have to tell him what I want, it doesn't count." Or, "I shouldn't have to ask." If you want to improve your circumstances, your job in your relationship is to take the lead and change the quality of your communication. Our relationships with men will never work if we wait for them to figure out what we want, any more than in business we can expect success without asking for what we want.

We forget how powerful we are and how easily our mates will go along with us if we tell them what we want, and they can get what they want, too. Too often, women expect our men to guess what's on our minds, know what we want, and how to give it to us. Except men are just not as intuitive as we are. They often don't pick up on those little nuances that come effortlessly to us.

He Needs to Feel Important and Necessary

Sherry and I met on the phone when she signed up for my ***Testosterone-Free Marketing*** teleclass. She opted for extra coaching. A bright, energetic woman from North Carolina, Sherry insisted her husband Doug of nineteen years was the problem. As a distributor for a major cosmetics company, she found herself pushing sales and business away when he would sigh, "You're leaving the house again?" She felt guilty and would miss opportunities for sales. Her husband was causing Sherry to sabotage her business.

When I first put the cause and effect together, and she saw what was happening, her reaction was sadness and anger. Why did Doug have to be so needy? Why couldn't he just give her the time and space she needed to do her thing? Most of the time when he came home from work, he sat behind the computer, engrossed in online computer games anyway. For years she was devoted and worked hard to home-school their two children. Now she felt it was her turn. She loved him but was frustrated. Sherry was blaming her husband, trying to get away from him rather than using her power to positively change the situation. Blaming always puts you in a "victim role" rather than in an empowered role.

Sherry was surprised when I suggested she be more sexually available to her husband. She laughed hysterically and said that was something she definitely could do. I felt a little funny giving this advice; after all, I'm a marketing coach not a relationship counselor. Her cavalier tone told me she was taking him for granted. He dealt with his feelings by withdrawing and giving her flak about her business. She responded by pulling away as well.

I told her, "Go to him and give him a hug and a kiss before you leave the house. Tell him when you'll be back rather than just yelling up the stairs, 'Byeee!' Tell him what you appreciate about him."

Sherry also told me has short, dark hair but her husband hinted that he'd like to see her as a blonde. "That is *not* going to happen!" she said angrily. "No way I'll deal with 'roots' every couple weeks."

The good news is, even after 19 years of marriage and two children, Sherry's husband visualizes her as a sexy blonde. I advised her, "If you like your short, dark hair, fine. Don't change it. Why not go to a wig shop and buy a long, blonde wig *only* for the bedroom so it becomes your little joke when the door is closed?" This wasn't the "marketing advice" she expected but I was suggesting she provide "excellent customer service."

She couldn't stop giggling. "Should I go to Fredericks and get a little outfit, too?" she asked.

"Hey, it's your marriage," I told her. "I'm a marketing coach, not a sex therapist. I just have a strong hunch it's going to work," I said. (One of my close friends has been married for 28 years. When I asked her why their marriage is so successful, she told me, "No matter how broke we've been, we always make sure there's money in our budget for Victoria's Secret.")

When Sherry started these changes with Doug three weeks ago, he started responding differently. When I talked to her on our fourth coaching call together, she and her husband were planning a vacation together without the kids for the first time in ten years. She gleefully told me that Doug had started calling her, "My Princess." Lately, it seems he couldn't give a hoot how busy she is with her business, as long as she takes an interest in him and makes time for him. Now that the relationship issues have been cleared up, I'm talking with her about the actual marketing strategies for her business. I knew that until then, any how-tos I gave her would result in disappointment because she would keep sabotaging her results.

After all, we marketed "our products and services" at the beginning of our relationships. It only makes sense that as time goes on, we need to continue to "service the account" to keep our most important customer happy and satisfied.

I'm not suggesting this "strategy" will work in every instance, but it's certainly worth the effort before letting your anger boil over or considering leaving a long term relationship. My relationship-wise friend Sue says men want three things: to be loved and appreciated, not to be made wrong, and, sex whenever they want it. Well okay, they'll wait until we want it too, if they are otherwise happy.

Our Rock of Gibraltar

A very sharp, observant man once told me he believes what women want is a man who is "unflappable." He meant steady, solid and emotionally available. The kind of guy around whom a woman will feel safe and secure. Every woman I have shared this thought with sighs, "Ohhhh ... yes! That's it."

We want a man who will be our "Rock of Gibraltar." We can trust he will be there for us no matter what. He doesn't pull away emotionally or explode at us. He may surprise us for our birthday, Valentine's Day, or just for fun. But there are no surprises in the unconditional support and love we get from him.

Many people get the message that if they fail, the people they love will leave them. Worse, many women get the message that if we succeed, the men we love will leave us. Every time a man behaves in a way that's threatened or insecure when we spend time on our business, the fear is, "If I'm successful, will he leave me because his ego can't handle it?" It's a double-bind that leaves many of us feeling we're in a Catch-22. Most of the time, what's happening is his concern not about how much money you make, but more about how important he still is in your eyes. As you start appreciating and valuing yourself more, it's important that you extend your appreciation to your partner just as you would want him to do.

My friend Steve said, "Love is the recognition, appreciation and encouragement of something unique and special in another." Obviously 'love' is not a possessive verb."

How Women Want to Be Supported

More men want to be supportive of their partners but they're not always sure how. And often what feels like support to men doesn't feel like support to women.

I'll never forget a self-growth seminar I attended about ten years ago. On the last day, we were asked to write down a 60-day goal. I decided to set a goal to lose weight. We picked three people to be our "support team." I chose two women and one man who I saw as a nice guy in previous exercises together. We were instructed to listen as the three people were to speak words of support and encouragement to us. We were supposed to just listen. The two women whispered how great I would look when I reached my goal weight and how much fun it would be to shop for attractive clothes. The man shouted in my ear, "Get up off your fat, lazy butt and get in that gym and sweat!" By the end of the three minute barrage, I was in tears. He was surprised. He honestly believed he was being supportive.

When many men attempt to support the woman they care about in her business, they say things like, "Hon, you gotta get out there and beat the bushes. Clobber the competition. You gotta go to war and beat them before they beat you. If you don't do that, you're not serious about your business." Unwittingly, his "words of support" are the very thing that terrifies us most. Go back and reread Chapter Eight to learn more. Because we're not built for "outwardly projecting," what we are told is exactly the opposite of our feminine nature.

What we need to hear is, "Hon, I believe in you. I love you just the way you are. And no matter what happens, I'll be here for you. Go for it!" That's it. No ninjas. No linebackers. No clobbering. When women use our "feminine force," we can create our own success our own way.

Recently I shared this message at a speaking engagement. The audience was half men and half women. A man came up to me and thanked me. "I finally got it," he said. "After your talk, I called my wife. I thought I was supporting her and she was just being lazy and not aggressive enough about marketing. Now I understand why she holds back. We had the first honest conversation about her business in a year."

Trust Her Intuitive Wisdom

Here's an analogy: In great, successful, positive relationships, men are the "ships" and women are the "radar." She knows she can counts on him to clear the way. And he knows he can count on her for her intuition.

A woman who wants the best for her relationship knows that it's important for him to trust her intuitive wisdom. Because our male and female brains are physically different and operate differently, foolish men have pooh-poohed our intuition throughout the centuries. There's an old saying: "Behind every successful woman is a man who's surprised as hell."

Wise men have relied upon our intuition for guidance and mutual support. As women, we often come to conclusions regarding what to do with a process that is less about rational thinking and much more about "feeling." Actually, linear thinking and analysis has failed many a man who "did the math," no matter how infallible it may have seemed.

Kimberly was an "Army brat" when she grew up. Her father accepted only linear, left-brained thinking from "his little girl." Nothing else mattered. "Non-rational thinking" was not to be trusted or relied upon. By shutting off her intuition as many of us do growing up in a left-brained world, Kimberly also shut off a large source of her power and wisdom as a woman. She started a business because it seemed practical, not because she had any passion for it. She decided to stop working in a business where she was unhappy and unfulfilled and really disliked her clients. She gradually learned to listen to those quiet urgings.

By taking a brief break, she learned she was more interested in creating a business where she could use her innate talents and express the creativity she had pushed down for so many years at her father's insistence. She now owns a business she loves and will thrive in. Kimberly is confident she will feel more at ease speaking passionately about what she does. That passion and fulfillment will make it easier for her to enjoy herself a lot more and create a lot more business.

If a "hyper-rational" man or anyone else has taught you to not trust your intuition, take the time to start listening again to that still, small voice inside. It is powerful and if you listen, it will not steer you wrong. Opening yourself to your intuition will open you to realize just how valuable it is when used daily in our world.

Take It Personally? It's Just Our Nature

When you're a kid in the neighborhood and you want to play baseball, you learn that it takes nine kids to make a baseball team. If you have only nine kids in the neighborhood who want to play ball, you take them all on your team even if you don't like every player personally, because for boys, it's more important to play ball than like everyone. That's one of the ways boys connect with their peers while growing up and as men.

For girls, the game is not as important as the relationships. In fact, relationships *are* the game. A girl will send her little friends home when she gets angry at them and then realizes she has no one to play with. But instead of calling her friends back, she simply won't play because the relationships are much more important than the game.

Boys learn valuable lessons about not taking things personally. "Business is business," they say. Many women take everything way too personally, but in the world of business, this can often be emotionally destructive. If a customer tries to dicker down our price, we take it personally rather than know he is just trying to get the best deal possible. Business relationships are still about business

This is one area where men can help us to see a situation in ways that are more beneficial to our success. Since men's brains are more compartmentalized, they separate issues more easily. The men in our lives can help us by showing us it's not always personal, and by not making us wrong for innately feeling that way. By developing a little thicker skin when it comes to business, you will be more at ease, less stressed and happier. Next time you feel upset with how someone handled a business transaction, talk with your partner about your feelings. He may be able to help you achieve the professional distance you need to not take things so personally all the time.

"Want Him To Be More of a Man? Try Being More of a Woman"

Being responsible for your side of the communication means not testing him to see if he passes or fails, but honestly and openly telling him what you want and why. If he wants you to be happy, chances are he will move heaven and earth to support you in getting it.

Back in the 1960s, long before feminists were telling us we had the same muscle strength and the same exact kind of thinking skills, the subheading above was an advertising slogan for a popular perfume. We now know that we are equals but in very different ways. When we begin to appreciate those differences, and the feelings, hopes and fears we have in common, we can truly enjoy this wonderful dance of loving and supporting each other. On the dance floor, he may lead and you follow, but in affairs of the heart, it's up to the woman to assume the lead even if it doesn't look that way to the outside observer.

Summing It Up

§ Men look to women to tell them how to support them in a relationship. It is up to you to tell the man you care about what you want in the relationship.

§ Relationship sabotage is when one person attempts, consciously or unconsciously, to undermine the other person's dreams and goals. When one person sabotages another, it is always because they feel threatened with the loss of power, of appreciation, of connectedness, and perhaps that they are "not enough."

§ Most men are not concerned how much time you spend on your business as long as he gets quality time and feels and believes that he is important and necessary to your happiness.

§ Women want a man who will be their "Rock of Gibraltar" and supportive through thick and thin. Many women get the message growing up that if she is successful, the man she loves will leave her.

§ The best kind of verbal support a man can give a woman is to say, "I believe in you and I'll be here for you no matter what happens."

§ Don't be dismissive of your intuitive wisdom. Help him trust your intuition, too.

§ He can be supportive by helping you to not take things so personally and having a little healthy detachment to events and circumstances. When he tells you, "It's just business, so don't take it personally," listen to him and learn.

Get Started Now

- How is the quality of your relationship? If everything is smooth sailing and you're blessed to have a relationship with a partner who supports and encourages you, consider yourself fortunate.
- Is he sabotaging you? Are you sabotaging him? Then you have unresolved and possibly unspoken issues. You cannot control or change another person … but you can control and change your own behavior. Get honest with yourself first. Stop doing or saying things that are less than loving and supportive. After all, isn't that what it means to be in love?
- Is he undermining your efforts by being needy and demanding? Perhaps he feels you are so caught up in your business that he's not important and your "knight in shining armor." Consider if the advice I gave to Sherry might work for you.
- You are more powerful in your relationship than you probably give yourself credit for. Take the responsibility for telling him what you want and need for you to be happy. Don't play games or make him guess. That's a lose-lose game.

- Is he physically or verbally abusive and you've been dancing on eggshells for years? You deserve to be happy, free and loved. If counseling and everything else you've done haven't worked and the advice above seems ludicrous, seek professional guidance about what your best options are. You may need to leave just to save your life.
- Trust your intuition and guidance and help him to see that, although the way you "feel" is different from how he "thinks," your intuitive knower is infallibly wise and worthy of your trust.
- Let him guide you to take things less personally when it's appropriate in business.

The Last Word

"Different" doesn't mean "lesser than"; it just means different.

Chapter Sixteen

Get in the Flow of Success

"You are searching for the magic key that will unlock the door to the source of power; and yet you have the key in your own hands, and you may use it the moment you learn to control your thoughts."

— Napoleon Hill

Real success has little to do with the how-tos, the mechanics or the step-by-step instructions you will find in other business and marketing books. "How to" is a weak question. It may provide information but you may feel that you still cannot do it. That's why I purposely did not get caught up in the mechanics and how-tos of marketing. Instead ***Testosterone Free Marketing*** is focused on the attitudes and mindset women business owners bring to marketing.

We can create the greatest success in our lives when we change our thoughts. Once you are open and willing to receive—a natural yin state for women—great ideas will rush to you.

We live in a mysterious Universe. Things happen and we simply have no logical explanation why. Scientists and mystics say most of reality happens at a level where we cannot see it with our own two eyes. There are countless examples of this deeper level of reality. Miracles happen every day and the biggest miracle is you. You have the ability to influence your outcomes and results, not just by what you do, but also by what you *think* about and imagine. Yes, you can create miracles with your thoughts.

A fairly new science called Quantum Physics is proving that what you think about comes about. Your dominant thoughts become your reality and it's never too late to make positive changes. Simply make new conscious choices. You have the power to change your life. You can change your cash flow, your marketing results, your relationships, your health, everything. It's not just positive thinking and putting a new spin on things. Most people have a little smidgen of positive thinking covering up a snake pit of negative thoughts, attitudes and ideas.

Change Your Thoughts - Change Your Results

If you were raised with the belief that it is noble to suffer and you bought into it, you will be provided with lots of opportunities to suffer. You can actually create disease in your body with your thoughts. This is not just my opinion; there are now numerous clinical research studies into the body-mind connection that prove it is true. (For more information, go to www.MarketingforHer.com, click on "Keyword" Search and then "Body-Mind Connection.")

What does this have to do with marketing your home-based business? Everything! If your beliefs do not support you deserving good things and great outcomes, you will not achieve them. Consider for a moment your beliefs about money and wealthy people. In Chapter Seven, I touched on the fact that most wealthy people are not unhappy, greedy or dishonest. You may not realize it on the surface – but if you believe wealthy or successful people are bad – you will never become one. Why would you want to become something you abhor?

Your core values and mindset must be in the right place for wealth to occur. If you believe you are not worthy or deserving of success, you either won't create it or you might create wealth and then lose it. All the marketing strategies, tips and ideas in the world won't amount to a hill of beans. Why? Because wealth and success are not in alignment with your Core Values. Remember our discussion of Core Values from Chapter Nine? Your Core Values drive who you are and what you become. And a low "Deservingness Quotient" will limit the abundance that can come into your life, which is why we often see winners of huge lottery amounts filing for bankruptcy a few years later.

Many organized religions teach their followers they are better, more righteous people for remaining in a state of never-ending striving and not arriving. (To discover how these beliefs started in the medieval days, go to www.MarketingforHer.com, click on "Keyword Search" and then "Divine Rights of Kings.") What do you believe about prosperity and wealth? What do you believe you deserve? Who taught you those lessons? Are you constantly careening from one financial or emotional headache to the next? Or are you flowing through life, trusting that success and the results you want always come to you?

Go back to the Clear Compelling Vision you wrote in Chapter Seven. Read it again. How do you feel when you read your words? Does it make you excited and vibrating with good feelings? Or do you have a sense of dread and disbelief?

How many of the statements below have you told yourself?

- "Who do you think you are?"
- "You'll never have what you want – so why even try?"
- "No matter what you do, people will say 'no,' so save your breath."
- "You don't deserve to be wealthy or successful."
- "Keep your nose to the grindstone and just be happy with what you have."
- "Don't get too big for your britches."
- "You might be poor, but at least you're happy."
- "Wealthy people are greedy, dishonest and unhappy."
- "We may not have much but at least we have each other."
- "Money is the root of all evil."
- "I don't want to bother with the stress rich people have."
- "If I have money, no one will love me for me."

If you are serious about success in your business and your life, but say any of these statements to yourself, start shifting your thinking.

Throughout this book you have discovered how your conditioning as a girl caused you to limit yourself and hold back when it comes to marketing your business. Marketing is about making connections and helping people achieve *their* dreams, while you achieve *yours* at the same time. If you stay conscious and present, you now have the power to make different conscious choices. If marketing has made you uneasy and anxious, this is one of the most significant lessons from this book.

Tiny Shifts Can Net Big Results

You wrote about your Perfect Day when you wrote your Clear Compelling Vision. What would it be like to have a Perfect Day today? Sure, the bills need to be paid and the dog threw up on your living room carpet. But what if you decided to approach an entire day with a positive, winning mindset? What would a day like that be like? At first, it can take a Herculean effort to be solution-oriented no matter what. A couple hours of "positive thinking" may leave you feeling it is unrealistic and Pollyanna-ish thinking. This is how successful people deal with problems and challenges. They do not enjoy the problems any more than you do. But they focus on finding solutions and they do it quickly rather than stew in "ain't it awful" thinking, as less successful people do.

When I was in my twenties and still fairly new into the full time world of work, I used to hop from one dramatic problem to another. Work problems, money problems, relationship problems, weight problems. I had them all. I fantasized about how great it would be when life settled down to "normal." A huge shift occurred when I realized daily stress and challenges *were* normal. How I responded to those stresses made the big difference. Okay, so I am starting to sound like a broken record now. It still goes back to making different conscious choices.

Vibrating at a Higher, More Passionate Level

When you feel positive, like a millionaire who hasn't deposited her checks yet, and you go for a morning walk, the air seems crisper and flowers more fragrant. Imagine your senses are heightened and you're vibrating at a higher level.

How does it feel when you put on a new blouse or sweater and you look great? Do you smile as you get compliments or admiring glances? You're more enthusiastic, passionate, and interested in what others say. The words "shy" or "self-conscious" are not part of your vocabulary when you feel this way.

Start operating from a higher energetic level. Choose to feel as if you had already achieved your goal. Post pictures of your vision in completed form around your home or office. Post positive affirmations on your bathroom mirror and on the dashboard of your car. Use affirmations that state who you are becoming as if you were already there, for example: "I am a confident, intelligent, outgoing woman and people love doing business with me." Combine high energy and positive expectations with ***Testosterone-Free Marketing*** strategies to help you reach your goals faster and make the process more fun.

When you operate at this high energy level, your goals are attracted to you like a magnet. Mysterious things shift that we cannot see but are still very real. You get in the flow of success and wealth. Your enthusiasm and joy are seen and felt by others. You communicate with passion about your business and how you help others. The perfect words come to you effortlessly. People want to be around others who love what they do. That's why people with those traits are often said to have a "magnetic personality."

When you operate from a higher vibrational place, you no longer make decisions from desperation, but from empowerment. You are unafraid to get your message out. You outwardly project and receive using both your yin and yang energy and have a great time doing it. You are in the flow of giving and receiving good. Don't insist on doing things the hard way if life gives you what you want without any fuss or muss. Always consider the possibility of a quantum leap. Sometimes you can develop a great plan on Friday and by Tuesday everything has changed. Be flexible. And remember the old saying, "Life is what happens when you're making other plans."

Recently I had a conversation with Paula. She was just starting as a real estate investor in the Chicago area. She found a house she was interested in buying but she was afraid the seller wouldn't accept her price and terms. She was meeting the seller the next day and confessed he was acting stand-offish on the phone. Maybe he did not want to sell his home after all. I reminded Paula she was in control. I asked her how an experienced real estate investor would behave in this situation. She told me that a seasoned real estate investor would behave as if there are lots of good deals out there, and that at any moment, she should be willing to get up and politely but firmly walk away.

Paula approached the meeting differently. She made different conscious choices. Instead of acting like a novice, her persona and energy were confident. Two days later, I received a call from Paula. She was so excited that I thought she would burst.

"What happened?" I asked.

She told me at one point in the negotiation, the seller became obstinate. Paula got up from the kitchen table and said, "I wish you well, but I just don't think we're going to be able to do business together." She walked out of the house toward her car, but before she opened the car door, the seller burst out of the house and caught up with her. He admitted he truly did want to sell his home, and convinced Paula to return to the table where they could come to an agreement at favorable terms. So suddenly everything shifted to help her get the deal she wanted.

When you market from a high vibrational place, your energy will catch the attention of others. It shows on the outside. You express a deeply felt part of who you are. You're authentic and real. So how do you keep that positive energy going?

Surround yourself with positive people, thoughts, and ideas. Look for positive solutions to the glitches that will occur from time to time. Have beautiful things to look at, whether you redecorate your office or place a vase of flowers or a flickering candle on your desk. Remove negative people from your life or, at least keep them at arm's length. Perhaps it sounds cruel, but as you become more positive, they will find you annoying anyway and try to drag you back to their comfort level. You will discover new friends who better reflect the person you're becoming.

We all want to improve our lives. You may want to start a business and increase your cash flow. Or, you may want to sell a business. In your personal life, you may want to resolve certain issues in your relationships. Maybe you want less stress and more time with family. If you are a home-based business owner, your job is helping your customers solve problems. The more customers you help and the more ways you help them, the more prosperous, and profitable you will be.

Testosterone-Free Tip: Life sometimes changes very quickly. Be open to manifesting and receiving effortlessly. Magic can occur when you meet the right people or are suddenly struck with the perfect idea or solution. Your intuition and creativity as a woman can be highly useful. Don't waste time questioning serendipity. Miracles happen every day.

Graphic is Good

Why do affirmations pale into nothing compared with visualizations? Studies have shown that for most people, the Subconscious Mind has the reasoning power of a three-year-old. Up until age three or so, it ran the show, but then your rational, reasoning Conscious Mind began to take over, leaving the Subconscious Mind behind in the shadows, stuck at age three.

However, if for some reason, the Conscious Mind is overwhelmed and paralyzed in indecision, not knowing what to do, the Subconscious Mind frequently takes over, often with disastrous results. Suppose someone gets upset at you and erupts for no apparent reason. Your Conscious Mind hasn't a clue what to do, so your Subconscious Mind retaliates with a snippy comment or thought that only makes things worse. Knowing that when people get upset, it is *never* about you but always about them, you can keep your cool and step in with your rational Conscious Mind, saying, "Gee, you're having a bad day. Can I do anything to help?"

At this point, the person may sadly share with you that his beloved four-year-old daughter has just been diagnosed with leukemia, and it doesn't look good. Or that he's just been diagnosed with cancer and is faced with chemotherapy. Or she may tell you that the husband she loves has just left her—it could be anything … except about you.

Why is the Subconscious Mind like this? In the early years, it simply recorded verbatim every piece of input it received, often misinterpreting that input. If a little girl was misbehaving and her mother said, "You should be ashamed of yourself," that input is recorded and stuck deep in her Subconscious Mind, completely unedited. Many years later, when someone makes a remark that pulls that memory to the surface, she suddenly finds herself feeling deeply ashamed but doesn't know why.

Children are excellent observers but they have poor skills when it comes to evaluating what they observe. One example is the child whose parents are divorcing and he or she believes that it must be because he was bad or naughty. Therefore, the contents of our Subconscious Mind rarely support us as adults. (Today, parents in the know play New Age music to the fetus by placing a speaker on the mother's abdomen, and speak encouraging words.) So the task facing us today is to bring the Subconscious Mind forward by providing it with new input that aligns with our rational Conscious Mind's decision-making. The challenge is that three-year-olds are not good with words, so affirmations are often an ineffective way to create positive change. However, at that age, we responded well to visual images—movies, TV, posters and pictures in books.

Cut out images from any source—women's magazines, home-and-garden magazines, even automobile brochures—that show people's needs being met. Surround yourself with these images. Go into relaxation mode daily and look at a photo of two people obviously in love and enjoying each other's company. As you do, repeat your affirmation, such as, "I have the perfect relationship." Or gaze at a picture of an obviously successful and happy woman for an affirmation about marketing success, such as, "I always get great results and make more money when I market my business."

Keep looking at the picture you chose and repeating the affirmation for 30 seconds or so. Then go on to the next picture and affirmation—maybe the perfect vehicle, business or body. Your Subconscious Mind doesn't have any physical senses of its own, so it doesn't know the difference between the actual experience and that image. It believes and remembers whatever it's told because that's its job.

Suppose you work with several men who frequently challenge your authority or expertise. If, as a little girl, your brothers always got the neat toys and privileges, and you were told, "You're just a girl," those challenges will cause you great stress because your Subconscious Mind's memories are undermining your Conscious Mind's agenda. Find a picture of a powerful-looking woman standing at the head of a conference table, addressing a roomful of men, who are looking at her with respect and admiration. As you gaze intently at this picture, say, "I am powerful, respected and admired."

Your Conscious Mind might be saying, "C'mon, gimme a break," but do you *really* know what's in your Subconscious Mind? If you don't, it will cost you only a couple minutes a day to find out. Do this for at least 21 days, and see what happens for you. If you forget to do your affirmations and visualizations for a day, start over and do it again for another 21 days. You will gradually find your self-esteem, confidence, abilities and success increasing. If you want to be richer, healthier, sexier, more popular, look and feel younger, or be a better lover, driver, artist, writer or anything, this technique can only help you and never hurt you.

Self-Discovery Questions: Who Are You?

There are unlimited choices and options available in life. So why do we keep creating the same results even when it is not serving our highest good? The questions below can help you identify your passions and grow them into a life and a business of meaning and purpose. The more passionate you feel, the less overwhelmed you will be about marketing your business. These questions can help you get to know you better and help you shift your business and your marketing to get into the flow of success without struggle.

- If you had the time, what would you most want to study, practice or master?
- What do you love to talk about and share with others?
- What skills or abilities do you do naturally receive compliments for?
- What interest do you seem constantly fascinated by?
- What one thing would you dare to do if you knew you could not fail?
- What specialized knowledge do people frequently ask you about?
- What crazy ideas about the future of your business and your marketing have you dismissed recently? Why?
- In what areas do you normally and effortlessly produce good results?
- What activities/skills tend to repeat themselves on this list?

Commitment Questions: How Committed Are You?

Your level of commitment can make a huge difference to your willingness to overcome hurdles in your business and really enjoy your successes. These questions will help you find out if you have you committed to your compelling vision. Commitment is the difference between living your vision now or one fictitious day in the future. Set your intention and watch what happens. This is how your business vision becomes your reality versus something unattainable that only happens for other people.

- Will you make a commitment to achieve the success you want?
- Will you face your fears, break disempowering habits and choose differently?
- Do you envision yourself as successful in your business (i.e., can you feel it, see it and describe it in great detail)?
- If you won the lottery tomorrow, would you still pursue your business?
- Is this something you feel you must do? Does it feel right to you?

Passion Questions: What Gets Your Juices Flowing?

In our society, we often ignore our special talents and choose our livelihood according to what feels "safe." Too often, however, what makes us feel safe does not fulfill us. Your soul has a deep desire to express itself in ways that bring you joy. These questions will help you to discover what that joy is and bring it out.

- What do you think about when you lie awake at night?
- What issues, needs, opportunities and ideas give you energy?
- What problems and challenges deeply concern you?
- What visions are almost impossible to get out of your head?
- What calling are you willing to give 100 percent of yourself to?

Integrity Questions: Who Are You Serving?

Your gifts can be used positively or negatively. Your challenge is to truthfully say, "I use my gifts and talents to enrich my life and the lives of others." As you grow more clear about why you chose to be a business owner, answer the following questions:

- Why do I honestly want to create a business?
- Am I doing this business for my own selfish reasons?
- Will I be able to use my highest gifts and talents?
- Will this business bring out the best in me?
- Will this business give me the opportunity to create a win-win?

Testosterone-Free Success

You now have the knowledge and the tools to be an amazing Testosterone-Free Marketer. Throughout these pages, you have learned that you don't have to be someone you're not to be a successful marketer and create more cash flow. You don't have to act like a man or be pushy and annoying to get customers to say "Yes."

Along the way you may have discovered that sharing your marketing message in an emotionally compelling way and with confidence requires a personal growth journey. To ignore that is to be inauthentic and not genuinely you. Your attitude, mindset and the emotional baggage you brought to your business before ***Testosterone-Free Marketing*** had a great deal to do with your lack of results and feelings of discomfort or anxiety. Being a business owner is often like a self-growth seminar every day. There is no hiding and the results of what you say and do have instant consequences – good or bad.

The conscious choices you make from this point forward will help you to market with greater confidence and connection to your Ideal Customer. It all stems from using the best of both your yin and yang qualities and traits. When your customers get your passion and how much you care about creating a win-win outcome, you will experience the success, freedom and fun you always knew your own business could provide.

As you market, be consciously aware of your actions and always, always be happy.

Summing It Up

§ Your thoughts create and maintain the reality you experience, so focus on only positive outcomes.

§ Successful people are not upbeat and positive because they're successful; they are successful because they are first upbeat and positive.

§ Stress is only stressful to the extent that you let it impact your body—raised adrenaline levels, higher pulse rate, etc. Enjoy a brisk walk, a workout or any other physical activity you enjoy.

§ The power of free will is the ability to choose; therefore success is a choice.

§ For those who think life has to be hard, it usually is, so just make a different choice.

§ If something looks too good to be true, it sometimes is, but always leave room for miracles.

Get Started Now

- If you're faced with a problem, take *one concrete step* towards resolving it *right now.* Don't stew in the problem; make a phone call, go on the Internet for more information, visit someone. *Just do something! And right now!*

- Decide to choose success over failure, and back it up with affirmations and positive images cut from magazines. If you want a particular make and model of car, get brochures from the dealership and display them prominently, telling yourself that the car is already yours. Your subconscious doesn't know the difference, and will begin to work with you on manifesting it.

- Get in the flow of abundance. Avoid people who tell you, "Life's hard and money's tight." Instead, mingle with those who have already made it and bask in their aura of success.

- If you've got a big presentation or difficult meeting coming up, rehearse it. Visualize the situation and pre-script a successful outcome, down to every little detail, including the feeling when you deposit that large check in the bank.
- Set aside a couple of hours in the next week, and go through the four questionnaires in this chapter, either alone or with a trusted friend who can give you honest feedback about you. (Remember that most people don't want you to change because that would pull them out of their comfort zone.) Then draw up a list of changes you want to make in your life, and implement one a week. When you do, reward yourself with something that makes you feel good.

Last Word:

Some day in the distant future, you will look back on your life. Choose *today* to have a lot to smile about on *that* day.

14

Printed in the United States
29748LVS00002B/69